Developed for busy lifestyles, this journal has just enough room
to capture five years' worth of reflections and insights
for every day of the year. These inspiring quotes and Bible verses
show us that, day in and day out, God is with us and speaks to us
through His Word, His creation, and His people.
We are encouraged to pay attention and take note.

Busy schedules don't often allow time for long journal entries.
Yet there is always time for a line or two of gratitude
or a note about a memorable moment: "Amazing sunrise today.
It was like God shining through to me." "Thanks for Amy, Lord.
She really helped me understand things." "Yesterday I felt like
work was just drudgery, Lord. And then today I saw why I am
where I am. How humbling."

Start any time. Write the calendar year in the space provided.
Jot down a thought, a revelation, a prayer, a discovery.
It is as easy as that. A simple note each day will create
a treasured collection of memories of how God
has been speaking to you all along.

January 1

Be still, and in the quiet moments, listen to the voice
of your heavenly Father. His words can renew your spirit...
no one knows you and your needs like He does.

JANET L. SMITH

20___ ....
....
....
....

20___ ....
....
....
....

20___ ....
....
....
....

20___ ....
....
....
....

20___ ....
....
....
....

January 2

We should be astonished at the goodness of God,
stunned that He should bother to call us by name,
our mouths wide open at His love, bewildered
that at this very moment we are standing on holy ground.

BRENNAN MANNING

20___ ....
....
....
....

20___ ....
....
....
....

20___ ....
....
....
....

20___ ....
....
....
....

20___ ....
....
....
....

January 3

To gently push aside and silence the many voices
that question my goodness and to trust that I will hear
the voice of blessing—that demands real effort.

HENRI J. M. NOUWEN

20___ ....
....
....
....

20___ ....
....
....
....

20___ ....
....
....
....

20___ ....
....
....
....

20___ ....
....
....
....

January 4

I will keep watch to see what He will speak to me.

HABAKKUK 2:1 NASB

20___ ....
....
....
....

20___ ....
....
....
....

20___ ....
....
....
....

20___ ....
....
....
....

20___ ....
....
....
....

January 5

Prayer is not asking. Prayer is putting oneself
in the hands of God, at His disposition, and listening
to His voice in the depth of our hearts.

MOTHER TERESA

20___ ....

....

....

....

20___ ....

....

....

....

20___ ....

....

....

....

20___ ....

....

....

....

20___ ....

....

....

....

January 6

One of the first things I usually ask God
when circumstances change is:
"God, is there something you want to teach me through this?"

REBECCA BARLOW JORDAN

20___ ....
....
....
....

20___ ....
....
....
....

20___ ....
....
....
....

20___ ....
....
....
....

20___ ....
....
....
....

January 7

Call to me and I will answer you.
I'll tell you marvelous and wondrous things
that you could never figure out on your own.

JEREMIAH 33:3 MSG

20___ ....
....
....
....

20___ ....
....
....
....

20___ ....
....
....
....

20___ ....
....
....
....

20___ ....
....
....
....

January 8

Prayer is spiritual communication between man and God,
a two-way relationship in which man
should not only talk to God but also listen to Him.

BILLY GRAHAM

20___ ....
....
....
....

20___ ....
....
....
....

20___ ....
....
....
....

20___ ....
....
....
....

20___ ....
....
....
....

January 9

"My thoughts are nothing like your thoughts," says the LORD.
"And my ways are far beyond anything you could imagine."

ISAIAH 55:8 NLT

20___

20___

20___

20___

20___

January 10

God's way of carrying out His plan may make no sense to us at all. But God is consistent. He does not change. His overall plan for each of His created beings will work.

RON EDMONDSON

20___ ....
....
....
....

20___ ....
....
....
....

20___ ....
....
....
....

20___ ....
....
....
....

20___ ....
....
....
....

January 11

When I called, you answered me;
you greatly emboldened me.

PSALM 138:3 NIV

20____ ....
....
....
....

20____ ....
....
....
....

20____ ....
....
....
....

20____ ....
....
....
....

20____ ....
....
....
....

January 12

Day-by-day as we listen, He's calling into being
facets of our design, character, and destiny that were previously
absent or missing. He's calling you into being all and everything He
had in mind before you were even born.

RUSTY RUSTENBACH

20___ ....
....
....
....

20___ ....
....
....
....

20___ ....
....
....
....

20___ ....
....
....
....

20___ ....
....
....
....

January 13

God whispers to us in our pleasures, speaks to us
in our conscience, but shouts in our pains:
It is His megaphone to rouse a deaf world.

C. S. Lewis

20___ ....
....
....
....
....

20___ ....
....
....
....
....

20___ ....
....
....
....
....

20___ ....
....
....
....
....

20___ ....
....
....
....
....

January 14

There is a God-shaped vacuum in every heart.

BLAISE PASCAL

20___

20___

20___

20___

20___

January 15

Certainly, people who pray are no more saints than the rest of us.
Rather, they are people who want to share a life with God,
to love and be loved, to speak and to listen, to work
and to be at rest in the presence of God.

ROBERTA BONDI

20___ ....
....
....
....

20___ ....
....
....
....

20___ ....
....
....
....

20___ ....
....
....
....

20___ ....
....
....
....

January 16

In him and through faith in him we may
approach God with freedom and confidence.

EPHESIANS 3:12 NIV

20___ ....
....
....
....

20___ ....
....
....
....

20___ ....
....
....
....

20___ ....
....
....
....

20___ ....
....
....
....

January 17

When I get quiet and lift my heart to God,
shutting out distractions, I hear His still small voice speaking words
of love to my heart, and I am filled with joy.

20___ ....
....
....
....

20___ ....
....
....
....

20___ ....
....
....
....

20___ ....
....
....
....

20___ ....
....
....
....

January 18

The goal of prayer is to live all of my life and speak all of my words
in the joyful awareness of the presence of God.

JOHN ORTBERG

20____ ....
....
....
....

20____ ....
....
....
....

20____ ....
....
....
....

20____ ....
....
....
....

20____ ....
....
....
....

January 19

Grant me, O Lord my God, a mind to know You,
a heart to seek You, wisdom to find You, conduct pleasing
to You, faithful perseverance in waiting for You,
and a hope of finally embracing You. Amen.

THOMAS AQUINAS

20____ ....

....

....

....

20____ ....

....

....

....

20____ ....

....

....

....

20____ ....

....

....

....

20____ ....

....

....

....

January 20

To be a Christian without prayer is no more possible
than to be alive without breathing.

MARTIN LUTHER KING JR.

20___ ....
....
....
....

20___ ....
....
....
....

20___ ....
....
....
....

20___ ....
....
....
....

20___ ....
....
....
....

January 24

My people, hear my teaching;
listen to the words of my mouth.

PSALM 78:1 NIV

20___

20___

20___

20___

20___

January 22

If you lower the ambient noise of your life and listen expectantly
for those whispers of God, your ears will hear them.
And when you follow their lead, your world will be rocked.

BILL HYBELS

20___ ....
....
....
....

20___ ....
....
....
....

20___ ....
....
....
....

20___ ....
....
....
....

20___ ....
....
....
....

January 23

He is a very creative God, and He likes to be highly creative in the various things He uses to communicate with us.

TERESA SEPUTIS

20___ ....
....
....
....
....

20___ ....
....
....
....
....

20___ ....
....
....
....
....

20___ ....
....
....
....
....

20___ ....
....
....
....
....

January 24

You may not be able to measure God's love,
but you can certainly experience it.

DILLON BURROUGHS

20____ ....

....

....

20____ ....

....

....

20____ ....

....

....

20____ ....

....

....

20____ ....

....

....

January 25

He gives more grace as our burdens grow greater,
He sends more strength as our labors increase;
To added afflictions He adds His mercy,
To multiplied trials He multiplies peace.

ANNIE JOHNSON FLINT

20___ ....
....
....
....

20___ ....
....
....
....

20___ ....
....
....
....

20___ ....
....
....
....

20___ ....
....
....
....

January 26

I will listen to what God the LORD says;
he promises peace to his people, his faithful servants.

PSALM 85:8 NIV

20___ ....
....
....
....

20___ ....
....
....
....

20___ ....
....
....
....

20___ ....
....
....
....

20___ ....
....
....
....

January 27

God's Word says He gives power to the weak and strength
to the powerless. In Him I can mount up on wings like an eagle,
rising above the stresses of my life.

20___ ....
....
....
....

20___ ....
....
....
....

20___ ....
....
....
....

20___ ....
....
....
....

20___ ....
....
....
....

January 28

In place of our exhaustion and spiritual fatigue,
God will give us rest. All He asks is that we come to Him…
that we spend a while thinking about Him, meditating on Him,
talking to Him, listening in silence.

CHARLES SWINDOLL

20___ ....
....
....
....

20___ ....
....
....
....

20___ ....
....
....
....

20___ ....
....
....
....

20___ ....
....
....
....

January 29

In Jesus the weak are strong, and the defenseless safe;
they could not be more strong if they were giants,
or more safe if they were in heaven. Faith gives to men on earth
the protection of the God of heaven.

CHARLES SPURGEON

20____ ....
....
....
....

20____ ....
....
....
....

20____ ....
....
....
....

20____ ....
....
....
....

20____ ....
....
....
....

January 30

Come and sit and ask Him whatever is on your heart. No question is too small, no riddle too simple. He has all the time in the world. Come and seek the will of God.

MAX LUCADO

20___ ....
....
....
....

20___ ....
....
....
....

20___ ....
....
....
....

20___ ....
....
....
....

20___ ....
....
....
....

January 31

Leave the hand open and be. Be at peace. Bend the knee
and be small and let God give what God chooses to give because
He only gives love and whisper a surprised thanks.

ANN VOSKAMP

20___ ....
....
....
....

20___ ....
....
....
....

20___ ....
....
....
....

20___ ....
....
....
....

20___ ....
....
....
....

February 1

Be still, and know that I am God.

PSALM 46:10 NKJV

20___ ....
....
....
....

20___ ....
....
....
....

20___ ....
....
....
....

20___ ....
....
....
....

20___ ....
....
....
....

February 2

We can't dash into God's presence and choke down spiritual inwardness before we hurry to our one o'clock appointment. Inwardness is time-consuming, open only to minds willing to sample spirituality in small bites, savoring each one.

CALVIN MILLER

20___ ....
....
....
....

20___ ....
....
....
....

20___ ....
....
....
....

20___ ....
....
....
....

20___ ....
....
....
....

February 3

God speaks to us through our desires. Then as we
lay them at his feet, he helps sort them out and quiets our hearts
to accept what He has already prepared.

ROSALIND RINKER

20___ ....
....
....
....

20___ ....
....
....
....

20___ ....
....
....
....

20___ ....
....
....
....

20___ ....
....
....
....

February 4

The LORD must wait for you to come to him
so he can show you his love and compassion.
For the LORD is a faithful God.
Blessed are those who wait for his help.

ISAIAH 30:18 NLT

20___ ....
....
....
....
....

20___ ....
....
....
....
....

20___ ....
....
....
....
....

20___ ....
....
....
....
....

20___ ....
....
....
....

February 5

There is not in the world a kind of life more sweet and delightful
than that of a continual conversation with God.

BROTHER LAWRENCE

20___ ....

....

....

20___ ....

....

....

20___ ....

....

....

20___ ....

....

....

20___ ....

....

....

February 6

God talks to His people—to each one of us—through His Word,
through the counsel of godly friends, and through the Holy Spirit.

SHEILA WALSH

20___ ....
....
....
....

20___ ....
....
....
....

20___ ....
....
....
....

20___ ....
....
....
....

20___ ....
....
....
....

February 7

My sheep listen to my voice;
I know them, and they follow me.

JOHN 10:27 NIV

20___ ....
....
....
....

20___ ....
....
....
....

20___ ....
....
....
....

20___ ....
....
....
....

20___ ....
....
....
....

February 8

God spoke, and life began. That same life-giving power
and creative force is at work when God
speaks to us in personal ways.

MARY YERKES

20___ ....
....
....
....

20___ ....
....
....
....

20___ ....
....
....
....

20___ ....
....
....
....

20___ ....
....
....
....

February 9

Prayer is not monologue, but dialogue; God's voice is its most essential part. Listening to God's voice is the secret of the assurance that He will listen to mine.

ANDREW MURRAY

20___ ....
....
....
....

20___ ....
....
....
....

20___ ....
....
....
....

20___ ....
....
....
....

20___ ....
....
....
....

February 10

God speaks to those who take the time to listen
and He listens to those who take the time to pray.

MARIO TOMASELLO

20___ ....
....
....
....
....

20___ ....
....
....
....
....

20___ ....
....
....
....
....

20___ ....
....
....
....
....

20___ ....
....
....
....

February 11

Prayer is the exercise of drawing on the grace of God.

OSWALD CHAMBERS

20___ ....
....
....
....

20___ ....
....
....
....

20___ ....
....
....
....

20___ ....
....
....
....

20___ ....
....
....
....

February 12

Since God knows our future, our personalities,
and our capacity to listen, He isn't ever going to say more to us
than we can deal with at the moment.

CHARLES STANLEY

20___ ....
....
....
....

20___ ....
....
....
....

20___ ....
....
....
....

20___ ....
....
....
....

20___ ....
....
....
....

February 13

The LORD is good and his love endures forever;
his faithfulness continues through all generations.

PSALM 100:5 NIV

20____

20____

20____

20____

20____

February 14

God wants to speak to us more than we want to listen.
He is a God of love, and love longs to communicate.

LINDA SCHUBERT

20___ ....
....
....
....

20___ ....
....
....
....

20___ ....
....
....
....

20___ ....
....
....
....

20___ ....
....
....
....

February 15

To love Him, you must love with all your heart.
You cannot be the person God meant you to be,
and you cannot live the life He meant you to live,
unless you live from the heart.

JOHN ELDREDGE

20____ ....
....
....
....

20____ ....
....
....
....

20____ ....
....
....
....

20____ ....
....
....
....

20____ ....
....
....
....

February 16

Retire from the world each day to some private spot....
Stay in the secret place till the surrounding noises begin to
fade out of your heart and a sense of God's presence envelops you.

A. W. TOZER

20___ ....
....
....
....

20___ ....
....
....
....

20___ ....
....
....
....

20___ ....
....
....
....

20___ ....
....
....
....

February 17

I need not shout my faith. Thrice eloquent
Are quiet trees and the green listening sod;
Hushed are the stars, whose power is never spent;
The hills are mute: yet how they speak of God!

CHARLES HANSON TOWNE

20___

20___

20___

20___

20___

February 18

In the morning, LORD, you hear my voice;
in the morning I lay my requests before you
and wait expectantly.

PSALM 5:3 NIV

20___ ....

....

....

....

20___ ....

....

....

....

20___ ....

....

....

....

20___ ....

....

....

....

20___ ....

....

....

....

February 19

The God who hears is also the one who speaks.
He has spoken and is still speaking…. He continues to speak
in ways that serious inquirers can hear if they will.

DALLAS WILLARD

20____ ....
....
....
....

20____ ....
....
....
....

20____ ....
....
....
....

20____ ....
....
....
....

20____ ....
....
....
....

February 20

Do not fear, for I am with you;
do not be dismayed, for I am your God.
I will strengthen you and help you;
I will uphold you with my righteous right hand.

ISAIAH 41:10 NIV

20____ ....
....
....
....

20____ ....
....
....
....

20____ ....
....
....
....

20____ ....
....
....
....

20____ ....
....
....
....

February 21

God is the sunshine that warms us, the rain that melts the frost and waters the young plants. The presence of God is a climate of strong and bracing love, always there.

JOAN ARNOLD

20___ ....
....
....
....

20___ ....
....
....
....

20___ ....
....
....
....

20___ ....
....
....
....

20___ ....
....
....
....

February 22

God wants you to know Him as personally as He knows you.
He craves a genuine relationship with you.

TOM RICHARDS

20_____ ....
....
....
....

20_____ ....
....
....
....

20_____ ....
....
....
....

20_____ ....
....
....
....

20_____ ....
....
....
....

February 23

The main thing that God asks for is our attention.

JIM CYMBALA

20___ ....
....
....
....

20___ ....
....
....
....

20___ ....
....
....
....

20___ ....
....
....
....

20___ ....
....
....
....

February 24

Worried about the future? Rest in God's promise that
He knows the plans He has for your life—
plans for good and not harm. He longs to bless you.

20___ ....
....
....
....

20___ ....
....
....
....

20___ ....
....
....
....

20___ ....
....
....
....

20___ ....
....
....
....

February 25

I believe God is managing affairs and that He doesn't
need any advice from me. With God in charge, I believe
everything will work out for the best in the end.
So what is there to worry about?

HENRY FORD

20___ ....

....

....

....

20___ ....

....

....

....

20___ ....

....

....

....

20___ ....

....

....

....

20___ ....

....

....

....

February 26

The Bible is a revelation of the mind and will of God to men.
Therein we may learn [who] God is.

JUPITER HAMMON

20___ ....
....
....
....

20___ ....
....
....
....

20___ ....
....
....
....

20___ ....
....
....
....

20___ ....
....
....
....

February 27

God speaks to us from His Word, the Bible. It...supplies His voice
in every area of our lives. It is the road map for your success at
school, work, in your marriage, with your friends, everything!

RON CHANNELL

20___ ....
....
....
....

20___ ....
....
....
....

20___ ....
....
....
....

20___ ....
....
....
....

20___ ....
....
....
....

February 28

How precious to me are your thoughts, God!
How vast is the sum of them!
Were I to count them,
they would outnumber the grains of sand.

PSALM 139:17–18 NIV

20___ ....
....
....
....

20___ ....
....
....
....

20___ ....
....
....
....

20___ ....
....
....
....

20___ ....
....
....
....

February 29

It's the little things that remind me of God's love,
that show me His presence and the sweet,
gentle touch of His concern and care for me.

Mia Pohlman

20___ ....
....
....
....

20___ ....
....
....
....

20___ ....
....
....
....

20___ ....
....
....
....

20___ ....
....
....
....

March 1

Your wisest moments will be those
when you say yes to God.

RICK WARREN

20___ ....
....
....
....

20___ ....
....
....
....

20___ ....
....
....
....

20___ ....
....
....
....

20___ ....
....
....
....

March 2

Listening to God is a firsthand experience…. God invites *you* to
vacation in His splendor. He invites *you* to feel the touch
of His hand. He invites *you* to feast at His table.
He wants to spend time with *you*.

MAX LUCADO

20___ ....
....
....
....

20___ ....
....
....
....

20___ ....
....
....
....

20___ ....
....
....
....

20___ ....
....
....
....

March 3

I pray that you, being rooted and established in love,
may have power...to grasp how wide and long and high
and deep is the love of Christ.

EPHESIANS 3:17–18 NIV

20___ ....
....
....
....

20___ ....
....
....
....

20___ ....
....
....
....

20___ ....
....
....
....

20___ ....
....
....
....

March 4

Prayer is essentially the expression of our heart longing for love.
It is not so much the listing of our requests but the breathing of our
own deepest request, to be united with God as fully as possible.

JEFF IMBACH

20___ ....
....
....
....

20___ ....
....
....
....

20___ ....
....
....
....

20___ ....
....
....
....

20___ ....
....
....
....

March 5

Great faith isn't the ability to believe long and far
into the misty future. It's simply taking God at His word
and taking the next step.

JONI EARECKSON TADA

20___ ....
....
....
....

20___ ....
....
....
....

20___ ....
....
....
....

20___ ....
....
....
....

20___ ....
....
....
....

March 6

Prayer is not so much an act as it is an attitude—
an attitude of dependency, dependency upon God.

ARTHUR PINK

20____ ....
....
....
....

20____ ....
....
....
....

20____ ....
....
....
....

20____ ....
....
....
....

20____ ....
....
....
....

March 7

The reflective life is a way of living that prepares the heart
so that something of eternal significance
can be planted there. Who knows what seeds may come to us,
or what harvest will come of them.

KEN GIRE

20___ ....
....
....
....

20___ ....
....
....
....

20___ ....
....
....
....

20___ ....
....
....
....

20___ ....
....
....
....

March 8

Listen, listen to me, and eat what is good,
and you will delight in the richest of fare.
Give ear and come to me;
listen, that you may live.

ISAIAH 55:2–3 NIV

20___ ....
....
....
....

20___ ....
....
....
....

20___ ....
....
....
....

20___ ....
....
....
....

20___ ....
....
....
....

March 9

There is no event so commonplace but that God
is present within it…always leaving you room to recognize Him
or not recognize Him, but all the more fascinatingly
because of that, all the more compellingly and hauntingly.

FREDERICK BUECHNER

20____ ....
....
....
....
....

20____ ....
....
....
....
....

20____ ....
....
....
....
....

20____ ....
....
....
....
....

20____ ....
....
....
....
....

March 10

People see God every day,
they just don't recognize him.

PEARL BAILEY

20___ ....
....
....
....

20___ ....
....
....
....

20___ ....
....
....
....

20___ ....
....
....
....

20___ ....
....
....
....

March 11

We must drink deeply from the very Source the deep calm and
peace of interior quietude and refreshment of God,
allowing the pure water of divine grace to flow plentifully
and unceasingly from the Source itself.

MOTHER TERESA

20____ ....
....
....
....

20____ ....
....
....
....

20____ ....
....
....
....

20____ ....
....
....
....

20____ ....
....
....
....

March 12

Just slipping quietly into the presence of God can be so exotic and fresh that it delights us enormously.

RICHARD J. FOSTER

20___

20___

20___

20___

20___

March 13

For those who have hidden fellowship with God,
life is a continuous feast.

S. G. DEGRAAF

20___ ....
....
....
....

20___ ....
....
....
....

20___ ....
....
....
....

20___ ....
....
....
....

20___ ....
....
....
....

March 14

You make known to me the path of life;
you will fill me with joy in your presence,
with eternal pleasures at your right hand.

PSALM 16:11 NIV

20___

20___

20___

20___

20___

March 15

God loves me just as I am today. He knows all my junk.
He knows all my inadequacies and lack of faith,
and He loves me anyway. However, He loves me too much
to leave me the way I am.

MICHELLE AKERS

20____ ....
....
....
....

20____ ....
....
....
....

20____ ....
....
....
....

20____ ....
....
....
....

20____ ....
....
....
....

March 16

Let your face shine on your servant;
save me in your unfailing love.

PSALM 31:16 NIV

20___ ....
....
....
....

20___ ....
....
....
....

20___ ....
....
....
....

20___ ....
....
....
....

20___ ....
....
....
....

March 17

May the sun shine warm upon your face,
May the rain fall soft upon your fields,
And, until we meet again,
May God hold you in the palm of His hand.

IRISH BLESSING

20___ ....
....
....
....

20___ ....
....
....
....

20___ ....
....
....
....

20___ ....
....
....
....

20___ ....
....
....
....

March 18

God Incarnate is the end of fear; and the heart that realizes that
He is in the midst, that takes heed to the assurance of His
loving presence, will be quiet in the midst of alarm.

F. B. MEYER

20___ ....
....
....
....

20___ ....
....
....
....

20___ ....
....
....
....

20___ ....
....
....
....

20___ ....
....
....
....

March 19

A quiet place is a good place to
find out God's angle on any problem.

JANETTE OKE

20___ ....
....
....
....

20___ ....
....
....
....

20___ ....
....
....
....

20___ ....
....
....
....

20___ ....
....
....
....

March 20

In quietness and confidence shall be your strength.

ISAIAH 30:15 NKJV

20___ ....
....
....
....

20___ ....
....
....
....

20___ ....
....
....
....

20___ ....
....
....
....

20___ ....
....
....
....

March 24

As Jesus stepped into the garden, you were in His prayers....
As Jesus dreamed of the day when we will be where He is,
He saw you there. His final prayer was about you.
His final pain was for you. His final passion was you.

MAX LUCADO

20___ ....
....
....
....

20___ ....
....
....
....

20___ ....
....
....
....

20___ ....
....
....
....

20___ ....
....
....
....

March 22

God's promises can never fail to be accomplished,
and those who patiently wait can never be disappointed.

L. B. COWMAN

20___ ....
....
....
....

20___ ....
....
....
....

20___ ....
....
....
....

20___ ....
....
....
....

20___ ....
....
....
....

March 23

If you receive a dream you believe is from God and if you don't
understand what He is saying, go back to God and ask Him….
Spend time with God discussing this dream
and ask Him to clarify it for you.

TERESA SEPUTIS

20___ ....
....
....
....

20___ ....
....
....
....

20___ ....
....
....
....

20___ ....
....
....
....

20___ ....
....
....
....

March 24

How rare it is to find a soul quiet enough to hear God speak.

FRANÇOIS FÉNELON

20___ ....
....
....
....

20___ ....
....
....
....

20___ ....
....
....
....

20___ ....
....
....
....

20___ ....
....
....
....

March 25

Blue skies with white clouds on summer days.
A myriad of stars on clear moonlit nights. Tulips and roses and
violets and dandelions and daisies. Bluebirds and laughter and
sunshine and Easter. See how He loves us!

ALICE CHAPIN

20_____ ....
....
....
....

20_____ ....
....
....
....

20_____ ....
....
....
....

20_____ ....
....
....
....

20_____ ....
....
....
....

March 26

Closet communion needs time for the
revelation of God's presence…. God knows how to save for you
the time you sacredly keep for communion with Him.

ARTHUR T. PIERSO

20___ ....
....
....
....

20___ ....
....
....
....

20___ ....
....
....
....

20___ ....
....
....
....

20___ ....
....
....
....

March 27

It's crucial that we keep a firm grip on
what we've heard so that we don't drift off.

HEBREWS 2:1 MSG

20____ ....
....
....
....

20____ ....
....
....
....

20____ ....
....
....
....

20____ ....
....
....
....

20____ ....
....
....
....

March 28

Blessed are those to whom Easter is not just a hunt...but a find;
Not just a greeting...but a proclamation;
Not just an outward fashion...but inward grace;
Not just a day...but an Eternity.

ANDERSON

20___ ....
....
....
....

20___ ....
....
....
....

20___ ....
....
....
....

20___ ....
....
....
....

20___ ....
....
....
....

March 29

[Sometimes] the soul converses with God
with a single loving glance.

CARLO CARRETTO

20___ ....
....
....
....

20___ ....
....
....
....

20___ ....
....
....
....

20___ ....
....
....
....

20___ ....
....
....
....

March 30

What does God think about us? His Word says
we are precious in His eyes and He loves us.

20___ ....
....
....
....

20___ ....
....
....
....

20___ ....
....
....
....

20___ ....
....
....
....

20___ ....
....
....
....

March 31

I am a flower quickly fading, here today and gone tomorrow,
a wave tossed in the ocean…. Still You hear me when I'm calling,
Lord; You catch me when I'm falling, and You've told me
who I am: I am Yours.

MARK HALL

20___ ....
....
....
....

20___ ....
....
....
....

20___ ....
....
....
....

20___ ....
....
....
....

20___ ....
....
....
....

April 1

God speaks to us through all of our senses.
His love often smells like spring rain, tastes like cinnamon toast,
and looks like a baby's sweet smile.

20___ ....
....
....
....

20___ ....
....
....
....

20___ ....
....
....
....

20___ ....
....
....
....

20___ ....
....
....
....

April 2

How many stanzas in the springtime breeze?
How plenty the raindrops? As He doth please,
There is no meter and there is no rhyme,
Yet God's poems always read in perfect time.

TERRI GUILLEMETS

20___

20___

20___

20___

20___

April 3

Not being changed by prayer is sort of like standing in the middle of a spring rain without getting wet. It's hard to stand in the center of God's acceptance and love without getting it all over you.

STEVE BROWN

20___ ....
....
....
....

20___ ....
....
....
....

20___ ....
....
....
....

20___ ....
....
....
....

20___ ....
....
....
....

April 4

Take a moment to consider the awesome reality that the God
who spoke and created the universe is now speaking to you.

HENRY T. BLACKABY

20___ ....
....
....
....

20___ ....
....
....
....

20___ ....
....
....
....

20___ ....
....
....
....

20___ ....
....
....
....

April 5

As the deer pants for streams of water,
so my soul pants for you, O God.
My soul thirsts for God, for the living God.

PSALM 42:1–2 NIV

20___ ....
....
....
....

20___ ....
....
....
....

20___ ....
....
....
....

20___ ....
....
....
....

20___ ....
....
....
....

April 6

Often God speaks through our quiet moments,
through other people, and through life's circumstances.

RON EDMONDSON

20____ ....
....
....
....

20____ ....
....
....
....

20____ ....
....
....
....

20____ ....
....
....
....

20____ ....
....
....
....

April 7

Spring bursts today,
For love is risen
and all the earth's at play.

CHRISTINA ROSSETTI

20___ ....
....
....
....

20___ ....
....
....
....

20___ ....
....
....
....

20___ ....
....
....
....

20___ ....
....
....
....

April 8

The wonder of living is held within the beauty of silence,
the glory of sunlight...the sweetness of fresh spring air,
the quiet strength of earth, and the love that lies
at the very root of all things.

20____ ....
....
....
....

20____ ....
....
....
....

20____ ....
....
....
....

20____ ....
....
....
....

20____ ....
....
....
....

April 9

How lovely is your dwelling place,
Lord Almighty!…
Better is one day in your courts
than a thousand elsewhere.

PSALM 84:1, 10 NIV

20___ ....
....
....
....

20___ ....
....
....
....

20___ ....
....
....
....

20___ ....
....
....
....

20___ ....
....
....
....

April 10

Easter spells out beauty,
the rare beauty of new life.

S. D. GORDON

20___ ....
....
....
....

20___ ....
....
....
....

20___ ....
....
....
....

20___ ....
....
....
....

20___ ....
....
....
....

April 11

A living, loving God can and does make His presence felt, can and does speak to us in the silence of our hearts, can and does warm and caress us till we no longer doubt that He is near, that He is here.

BRENNAN MANNING

20___ ....
....
....
....

20___ ....
....
....
....

20___ ....
....
....
....

20___ ....
....
....
....

20___ ....
....
....
....

April 12

He is the Source. Of everything. Strength for your day.
Comfort for your soul. Grace for your battle.
Provision for each need. Understanding for each failure.
Assistance for every encounter.

JACK HAYFORD

20___ ....
....
....
....

20___ ....
....
....
....

20___ ....
....
....
....

20___ ....
....
....
....

20___ ....
....
....
....

April 13

Sometimes while praying, God's Spirit will remind us
of a Scripture or a truth in His Word that we can
directly apply to the situation.

REBECCA BARLOW JORDAN

20___ ....
....
....
....

20___ ....
....
....
....

20___ ....
....
....
....

20___ ....
....
....
....

20___ ....
....
....
....

April 14

We have a Father in heaven who is almighty,
who loves His children…and whose very joy and delight it is to…
help them at all times.

GEORGE MUELLER

20___ ....
....
....
....

20___ ....
....
....
....

20___ ....
....
....
....

20___ ....
....
....
....

20___ ....
....
....
....

April 15

Let the beloved of the LORD rest secure in him,
for he shields him all day long,
and the one the LORD loves rests between his shoulders.

DEUTERONOMY 33:12 NIV

20___ ....
....
....
....

20___ ....
....
....
....

20___ ....
....
....
....

20___ ....
....
....
....

20___ ....
....
....
....

April 16

Joy is...deeper than an emotional expression of happiness.
Joy is a growing, evolving manifestation of God in my life
as I walk with Him.

BONNIE MONSON

20___ ....
....
....
....
....

20___ ....
....
....
....
....

20___ ....
....
....
....
....

20___ ....
....
....
....
....

20___ ....
....
....
....
....

April 17

God is more anxious to bless us than we are to be blessed.
More anxious to give us wisdom, strength, and peace
than we are to take them.

RICHARD C. HALVERSON

20___ ....
....
....
....

20___ ....
....
....
....

20___ ....
....
....
....

20___ ....
....
....
....

20___ ....
....
....
....

April 18

No eye has seen, no ear has heard,
and no mind has imagined
what God has prepared
for those who love him.

1 CORINTHIANS 2:9 NLT

20___ ....
....
....
....

20___ ....
....
....
....

20___ ....
....
....
....

20___ ....
....
....
....

20___ ....
....
....
....

April 19

We aren't just thrown on this earth like dice tossed across a table.
We are lovingly placed here for a purpose.

CHARLES SWINDOLL

20___ ....
....
....
....

20___ ....
....
....
....

20___ ....
....
....
....

20___ ....
....
....
....

20___ ....
....
....
....

April 20

Are you weak? Weary? Confused? Troubled? Pressured?
How is your relationship with God? Is it held
in its place of priority? I believe the greater the pressure,
the greater your need for time alone with Him.

KAY ARTHUR

20___ ....
....
....
....

20___ ....
....
....
....

20___ ....
....
....
....

20___ ....
....
....
....

20___ ....
....
....
....

April 21

Time spent alone with God is not wasted. It changes us;
it changes our surroundings; and every Christian
who would live the life that counts, and who would have power
for service must take time to pray.

MATILDA E. ANDROSS

20___ ....
....
....
....

20___ ....
....
....
....

20___ ....
....
....
....

20___ ....
....
....
....

20___ ....
....
....
....

April 22

We tend to be preoccupied by our problems when we have a
heightened sense of vulnerability and a diminished sense of power.
Today, see each problem as an invitation to prayer.

JOHN ORTBERG

20___ ....

....

....

....

20___ ....

....

....

....

20___ ....

....

....

....

20___ ....

....

....

....

20___ ....

....

....

....

April 23

Trust in the LORD with all your heart,
And lean not on your own understanding;
In all your ways acknowledge Him,
And He shall direct your paths.

PROVERBS 3:5–6 NKJV

20___ ....
....
....
....

20___ ....
....
....
....

20___ ....
....
....
....

20___ ....
....
....
....

20___ ....
....
....
....

April 24

God usually answers our prayers so much more according to the measure of His own magnificence than of our asking, that we do not recognize His benefits to be those for which we sought Him.

COVENTRY PATMORE

20___ ....
....
....
....

20___ ....
....
....
....

20___ ....
....
....
....

20___ ....
....
....
....

20___ ....
....
....
....

April 25

Make within our hearts a quiet place. We release to You our demand to see what the future holds. We rest in You, content to know only You and care in this present hour.

PETER MARSHALL

20___ ....
....
....
....

20___ ....
....
....
....

20___ ....
....
....
....

20___ ....
....
....
....

20___ ....
....
....
....

April 26

God is kind.... In kindness he takes us firmly by the hand
and leads us into a radical life-change.

ROMANS 2:4 MSG

20___ ....
....
....
....
....

20___ ....
....
....
....
....

20___ ....
....
....
....
....

20___ ....
....
....
....
....

20___ ....
....
....
....

April 27

A life contemplating the blessings of Christ
becomes a life acting the love of Christ.

ANN VOSKAMP

20___ ....
....
....
....

20___ ....
....
....
....

20___ ....
....
....
....

20___ ....
....
....
....

20___ ....
....
....
....

April 28

For [God] is, indeed, a wonderful Father who longs to pour out His mercy upon us, and whose majesty is so great that He can transform us from deep within.

TERESA OF ÁVILA

20____ ....
....
....
....

20____ ....
....
....
....

20____ ....
....
....
....

20____ ....
....
....
....

20____ ....
....
....
....

April 29

The surprisingly wonderful thing about my new adventure of
listening to God was that God, my Perfect Father, called me out to
be the person He'd created me to be.

RUSTY RUSTENBACH

20___ ....
....
....
....

20___ ....
....
....
....

20___ ....
....
....
....

20___ ....
....
....
....

20___ ....
....
....
....

April 30

You have made us for Yourself, O Lord, and our heart
is restless until it rests in You.

AUGUSTINE

20____ ....

....

....

....

20____ ....

....

....

....

20____ ....

....

....

....

20____ ....

....

....

....

20____ ....

....

....

....

May 1

We have a tremendous treasure in nature and will realize that it is holy and sacred. We will see God reaching out to us in every wind that blows, every sunrise and sunset, every cloud in the sky, every flower that blooms, and every leaf that fades.

OSWALD CHAMBERS

20___ ....
....
....
....

20___ ....
....
....
....

20___ ....
....
....
....

20___ ....
....
....
....

20___ ....
....
....
....

May 2

Learn to worship God as the God who does wonders, who wishes
to prove in you that He can do something supernatural and divine.

ANDREW MURRAY

20___ ....
....
....
....

20___ ....
....
....
....

20___ ....
....
....
....

20___ ....
....
....
....

20___ ....
....
....
....

May 3

True prayer is simply a quiet, sincere,
genuine conversation with God.
It is a two-way dialogue between friends.

W. PHILLIP KELLER

20___ ....
....
....
....

20___ ....
....
....
....

20___ ....
....
....
....

20___ ....
....
....
....

20___ ....
....
....
....

May 4

God…we invite you now to come into our national life.
We put our trust in you. We have our "Trust in God"
on our coins—we need to practice it.

ANNE GRAHAM LOTZ

20___ ....
....
....
....

20___ ....
....
....
....

20___ ....
....
....
....

20___ ....
....
....
....

20___ ....
....
....
....

May 5

When you pray, go away by yourself, shut the door behind you,
and pray to your Father in private. Then your Father,
who sees everything, will reward you.

MATTHEW 6:6 NLT

20___ ....
....
....
....

20___ ....
....
....
....

20___ ....
....
....
....

20___ ....
....
....
....

20___ ....
....
....
....

May 6

God sometimes seems to speak to us most intimately
when He catches us, as it were, off our guard.

C. S. Lewis

20___ ....
....
....
....

20___ ....
....
....
....

20___ ....
....
....
....

20___ ....
....
....
....

20___ ....
....
....
....

May 7

When I'm fearful, God's Word tells me I don't need to be afraid;
He has called me by name and I belong to Him.

20___ ....
....
....
....

20___ ....
....
....
....

20___ ....
....
....
....

20___ ....
....
....
....

20___ ....
....
....
....

May 8

In a world of so many uncertainties, economic crisis,
mortgage crisis, unemployment, fears, anxiety, worry,
hurt and pain, I hear God saying "Trust Me!"

DEBRA AIKEN

20____ ....
....
....
....

20____ ....
....
....
....

20____ ....
....
....
....

20____ ....
....
....
....

20____ ....
....
....
....

May 9

If you have a mom, there is nowhere you are likely to go
where a prayer has not already been.

ROBERT BRAULT

20___ ....
....
....
....

20___ ....
....
....
....

20___ ....
....
....
....

20___ ....
....
....
....

20___ ....
....
....
....

May 10

I love the LORD because he hears my voice
and my prayer for mercy.
Because he bends down to listen,
I will pray as long as I have breath!

PSALM 116:1–2 NLT

20___ ....
....
....
....

20___ ....
....
....
....

20___ ....
....
....
....

20___ ....
....
....
....

20___ ....
....
....
....

May 11

No one can fully measure the blessings that come to the life
of the one who has a praying mother.

ROY LESSIN

20___ ....
....
....
....

20___ ....
....
....
....

20___ ....
....
....
....

20___ ....
....
....
....

20___ ....
....
....
....

May 12

When I walk by the wayside, He is along with me.
When I enter into company amid all my forgetfulness of Him,
He never forgets me.

THOMAS CHALMERS

20____ ....
....
....
....

20____ ....
....
....
....

20____ ....
....
....
....

20____ ....
....
....
....

20____ ....
....
....
....

May 13

Faith comes alive when the Word read from the page
becomes the Word heard in your heart.

Rex Rouis

20___ ....
....
....
....

20___ ....
....
....
....

20___ ....
....
....
....

20___ ....
....
....
....

20___ ....
....
....
....

May 14

I love to think of nature as an unlimited broadcasting station
through which God speaks to us every hour,
if only we will tune in.

GEORGE WASHINGTON CARVER

20___ ....
....
....
....

20___ ....
....
....
....

20___ ....
....
....
....

20___ ....
....
....
....

20___ ....
....
....
....

May 15

I urge you to pray for absolutely everything, ranging from small to large. Include everything as you embrace this God-life, and you'll get God's everything.

MARK 11:24 MSG

20___ ....

....

....

....

20___ ....

....

....

20___ ....

....

....

20___ ....

....

....

20___ ....

....

....

....

May 16

As you sit quietly in My Presence remember
I am a God of abundance. I will never run out of resources;
My capacity to bless you is unlimited.

SARAH YOUNG

20___ ....
....
....
....

20___ ....
....
....
....

20___ ....
....
....
....

20___ ....
....
....
....

20___ ....
....
....
....

May 17

Wait before the Lord. Wait in the stillness. And in that stillness,
assurance will come to you. You will know that you are heard…
you will hear quiet words spoken to you yourself,
perhaps to your grateful surprise and refreshment.

AMY CARMICHAEL

20___ ....
....
....
....

20___ ....
....
....
....

20___ ....
....
....
....

20___ ....
....
....
....

20___ ....
....
....
....

May 18

The God who created, names, and numbers the stars
in the heavens also numbers the hairs of my head.... He pays
attention to very big things and to very small ones. What matters
to me matters to Him, and that changes my life.

ELISABETH ELLIOT

20___ ....
....
....
....

20___ ....
....
....
....

20___ ....
....
....
....

20___ ....
....
....
....

20___ ....
....
....
....

May 19

Know that the LORD is God.
It is he who made us, and we are his;
we are his people, the sheep of his pasture.

PSALM 100:3 NIV

20___ ....
....
....
....

20___ ....
....
....
....

20___ ....
....
....
....

20___ ....
....
....
....

20___ ....
....
....
....

May 20

Only God gives true peace—a quiet gift He sets within us just
when we think we've exhausted our search for it.

20____ ....
....
....
....

20____ ....
....
....
....

20____ ....
....
....
....

20____ ....
....
....
....

20____ ....
....
....
....

May 21

It takes deliberate and continuous effort to carve out time in our
overfull schedules to listen to the voice of God.

SHEILA WALSH

20____ ....
....
....
....

20____ ....
....
....
....

20____ ....
....
....
....

20____ ....
....
....
....

20____ ....
....
....
....

May 22

We sometimes fear to bring our troubles to God, because they
must seem so small to Him who sits on the circle of the earth.
But if they are large enough to concern and endanger our welfare,
they are large enough to touch His heart of love.

R. A. TORREY

20___ ....
....
....
....

20___ ....
....
....
....

20___ ....
....
....
....

20___ ....
....
....
....

20___ ....
....
....
....

May 23

Find a peaceful spot in nature and quiet your spirit.
Lift your heart to God and listen for His still, small voice.

20___ ....
....
....
....

20___ ....
....
....
....

20___ ....
....
....
....

20___ ....
....
....
....

20___ ....
....
....
....

May 24

God can be and wants to be found in everything we do.
In every moment of life, God is waiting to reveal himself to us
and fulfill us through the revelation of who he is.

MIA POHLMAN

20____ ....
....
....
....

20____ ....
....
....
....

20____ ....
....
....
....

20____ ....
....
....
....

20____ ....
....
....
....

May 25

Often times God wants us to sit before Him in quietness.
He doesn't want us to do all the talking.

CHARLES STANLEY

20___

20___

20___

20___

20___

May 26

God speaks to me in very small ways and sometimes
with what seem to be just ordinary impulses.
I've learned to listen to God's voice in the ordinary.

L. T. H.

20___ ....
....
....
....

20___ ....
....
....
....

20___ ....
....
....
....

20___ ....
....
....
....

20___ ....
....
....
....

May 27

Sit by the lake's edge, listening to the water lapping the shore, and hear your Father gently calling you to that place near His heart.

WENDY MOORE

20____ ....
....
....
....

20____ ....
....
....
....

20____ ....
....
....
....

20____ ....
....
....
....

20____ ....
....
....
....

May 28

Through everything God made, we can clearly
see his invisible qualities, his eternal power and divine nature.
Therefore, the Bible tells us that if we look, we'll see God speak.

RON CHANNELL

20____ ....
....
....
....

20____ ....
....
....
....

20____ ....
....
....
....

20____ ....
....
....
....

20____ ....
....
....
....

May 29

The heavens proclaim the glory of God.
The skies display his craftsmanship.
Day after day they continue to speak;
night after night they make him known.

PSALM 19:1-2 NLT

20___ ....
....
....
....

20___ ....
....
....
....

20___ ....
....
....
....

20___ ....
....
....
....

20___ ....
....
....
....

May 30

If you wish to know God, you must know His Word....
If you wish to know His purpose before it comes to pass,
you can only discover it by His Word.

CHARLES SPURGEON

20____ ....
....
....
....

20____ ....
....
....
....

20____ ....
....
....
....

20____ ....
....
....
....

20____ ....
....
....
....

May 31

God is never in a hurry,
but he is always on time.

RICK WARREN

20____ ....
....
....
....

20____ ....
....
....
....

20____ ....
....
....
....

20____ ....
....
....
....

20____ ....
....
....

June 1

To You, O LORD, I lift up my soul. O my God, I trust in You....
Show me Your ways, O LORD; teach me Your paths.

PSALM 25:1–2, 4 NKJV

20____ ....
....
....
....

20____ ....
....
....
....

20____ ....
....
....
....

20____ ....
....
....
....

20____ ....
....
....
....

June 2

To hear God we need to listen carefully. Whispers.
Impressions. Images. Hunches and thoughts that spring forth.
Dreams and longings of the heart. These are some of the subtle
but direct ways…God speaks to us today.

BILL GAULTIERE

20___ ....
....
....
....

20___ ....
....
....
....

20___ ....
....
....
....

20___ ....
....
....
....

20___ ....
....
....
....

June 3

What difficulty or challenge are you dealing with right now?
Bring it to the Lord and ask Him to show you the way.
He loves to give wisdom to anyone who asks!

20___ ....
....
....
....

20___ ....
....
....
....

20___ ....
....
....
....

20___ ....
....
....
....

20___ ....
....
....
....

June 4

Never be afraid to trust an unknown future to a known God.

CORRIE TEN BOOM

20___ ....
....
....
....

20___ ....
....
....
....

20___ ....
....
....
....

20___ ....
....
....
....

20___ ....
....
....
....

June 5

The Advocate, the Holy Spirit, whom the Father
will send in my name, will teach you all things and will
remind you of everything I have said to you.

JOHN 14:26 NIV

20___ ....
....
....
....

20___ ....
....
....
....

20___ ....
....
....
....

20___ ....
....
....
....

20___ ....
....
....
....

June 6

Even though you may not understand
how God works, you know He does.

MAX LUCADO

20___ ....
....
....
....

20___ ....
....
....
....

20___ ....
....
....
....

20___ ....
....
....
....

20___ ....
....
....
....

June 7

I would rather walk with God
in the dark than go alone in the light.

MARY GARDINER BRAINARD

20___ ....
....
....
....

20___ ....
....
....
....

20___ ....
....
....
....

20___ ....
....
....
....

20___ ....
....
....
....

June 8

Think of a time when God spoke to you through a friend.
What words of wisdom or comfort did He impart?

20____ ....
....
....
....
....

20____ ....
....
....
....
....

20____ ....
....
....
....
....

20____ ....
....
....
....
....

20____ ....
....
....
....
....

June 9

Oh, the depth of the riches of the wisdom and knowledge of God!
How unsearchable his judgments, and his paths beyond tracing out!

ROMANS 11:33 NIV

20___ ....
....
....
....

20___ ....
....
....
....

20___ ....
....
....
....

20___ ....
....
....
....

20___ ....
....
....
....

June 10

A father's influence is important because
it helps a child to love God, the heavenly Father,
if he respects his earthly father.

BILL GLASS

20____ ....
....
....
....

20____ ....
....
....

20____ ....
....
....
....

20____ ....
....
....
....

20____ ....
....
....

June 11

God speaks to me not through the thunder and the earthquake, not through the ocean and the stars, but through the Son of Man, and speaks in a language adapted to the imperfect sight and hearing.

WILLIAM LYON PHELPS

20___ ....
....
....
....

20___ ....
....
....
....

20___ ....
....
....
....

20___ ....
....
....
....

20___ ....
....
....
....

June 12

Incredible as it may seem, God wants...to be a father to us,
to shield us, to protect us, to counsel us,
and to guide us in our way through life.

BILLY GRAHAM

20___ ....
....
....
....

20___ ....
....
....
....

20___ ....
....
....
....

20___ ....
....
....
....

20___ ....
....
....
....

June 13

There are four ways God answers prayer:
No, not yet; No, I love you too much;
Yes, I thought you'd never ask; Yes, and here's more.

ANNE LEWIS

20___ ....
....
....
....

20___ ....
....
....
....

20___ ....
....
....
....

20___ ....
....
....
....

20___ ....
....
....
....

June 14

Nothing can separate you from God's love, absolutely nothing.
God is enough for time, God is enough for eternity. God is enough!

HANNAH WHITALL SMITH

20___ ....
....
....
....

20___ ....
....
....
....

20___ ....
....
....
....

20___ ....
....
....
....

20___ ....
....
....
....

June 15

As a father has compassion on his children,
so the LORD has compassion on those who fear him;
for he knows how we are formed,
he remembers that we are dust.

PSALM 103:13–14 NIV

20___ ....
....
....
....

20___ ....
....
....
....

20___ ....
....
....
....

20___ ....
....
....
....

20___ ....
....
....
....

June 16

God is a rich and bountiful Father, and He does not
forget His children, nor withhold from them anything which it
would be to their advantage to receive.

J. K. MACLEAN

20___ ....
....
....
....

20___ ....
....
....
....

20___ ....
....
....
....

20___ ....
....
....
....

20___ ....
....
....
....

June 17

Jesus knows when a request comes to Him from the heart.
He has been waiting all along for us to bring our needy selves
to Him and receive from Him that eternal water.

DORIS GAILEY

20_____ ....
....
....
....

20_____ ....
....
....
....

20_____ ....
....
....
....

20_____ ....
....
....
....

20_____ ....
....
....
....

June 18

From the ends of the earth I call to you,
I call as my heart grows faint;
lead me to the rock that is higher than I.
For you have been my refuge.

PSALM 61:2–3 NIV

20___

20___

20___

20___

20___

June 19

We ought to act with God in the greatest simplicity,
speak to Him frankly and plainly,
and implore His assistance in our affairs.

BROTHER LAWRENCE

20___ ....
....
....
....

20___ ....
....
....
....

20___ ....
....
....
....

20___ ....
....
....
....

20___ ....
....
....
....

June 20

Prayer at its highest is a two-way conversation—and for me
the most important part is listening to God's replies.

FRANK C. LAUBACH

20____ ....
....
....
....

20____ ....
....
....
....

20____ ....
....
....
....

20____ ....
....
....
....

20____ ....
....
....
....

June 21

The best remedy for those who are afraid, lonely,
or unhappy is to go outside, somewhere where they can be quiet,
alone with the heavens, nature, and God. Because only then does
one feel that all is as it should be.

ANNE FRANK

20____ ....
....
....
....

20____ ....
....
....
....

20____ ....
....
....
....

20____ ....
....
....
....

20____ ....
....
....
....

June 22

Teach me how to quiet my racing, rising heart
So I might hear the answer You are trying to impart.

HELEN STEINER RICE

20____ ....
....
....
....

20____ ....
....
....
....

20____ ....
....
....
....

20____ ....
....
....
....

20____ ....
....
....
....

June 23

Bestow upon us...O Lord our God, understanding to know you,
diligence to seek you, wisdom to find you, and a faithfulness that
may finally embrace you.

THOMAS AQUINAS

20___ ....
....
....
....

20___ ....
....
....
....

20___ ....
....
....
....

20___ ....
....
....
....

20___ ....
....
....
....

June 24

Ask and it will be given to you; seek and you will find;
knock and the door will be opened to you.

LUKE 11:9 NIV

20____ ....
....
....
....
....

20____ ....
....
....
....
....

20____ ....
....
....
....
....

20____ ....
....
....
....
....

20____ ....
....
....
....

June 25

He speaks, and the sound of His voice
Is so sweet the birds hush their singing,
And the melody that He gave to me
Within my heart is ringing.

C. Austin Miles

20____ ....
....
....
....

20____ ....
....
....
....

20____ ....
....
....
....

20____ ....
....
....
....

20____ ....
....
....
....

June 26

The silence of prayer is the silence of listening.

ELIZABETH O'CONNOR

20___ ....
....
....
....

20___ ....
....
....
....

20___ ....
....
....
....
....

20___ ....
....
....
....
....

20___ ....
....
....
....

June 27

When I'm exhausted before the day is half spent,
the Lord beckons, "Come to Me,
and I will give you rest."

20___ ....
....
....
....

20___ ....
....
....
....

20___ ....
....
....
....

20___ ....
....
....
....

20___ ....
....
....
....

June 28

God is not only the answer to a thousand needs.
He is the answer to a thousand wants. He is the fulfillment
of our chief desire in all of life.

BETH MOORE

20___ ....
....
....
....

20___ ....
....
....
....

20___ ....
....
....
....

20___ ....
....
....
....

20___ ....
....
....
....

June 29

I am graven on the palms of His hands.
I am never out of His mind. All my knowledge of Him
depends on His sustained initiative in knowing me.

J. I. PACKER

20____ ....
....
....
....

20____ ....
....
....
....

20____ ....
....
....
....

20____ ....
....
....
....

20____ ....
....
....
....

June 30

Never doubt in the dark
what God has shown you in the light.

EDITH EDMAN

20___ ....
....
....
....

20___ ....
....
....
....

20___ ....
....
....
....

20___ ....
....
....
....

20___ ....
....
....
....

July 1

Faith is the bucket of power lowered by the rope of prayer into the well of God's abundance. What we bring up depends upon what we let down. We have every encouragement to use a big bucket.

VIRGINIA WHITMAN

20___ ....
....
....
....

20___ ....
....
....
....

20___ ....
....
....
....

20___ ....
....
....
....

20___ ....
....
....
....

July 2

Now to him who is able to do immeasurably more than all we ask
or imagine, according to his power that is at work within us,
to him be glory...for ever and ever!

EPHESIANS 3:20–21 NIV

20____

20____

20____

20____

20____

July 3

We walk without fear, full of hope and courage
and strength to do His will, waiting for the endless good
which He is always giving as fast as He can get us able to take it in.

GEORGE MACDONALD

20___ ....
....
....
....

20___ ....
....
....
....

20___ ....
....
....
....

20___ ....
....
....
....

20___ ....
....
....
....

July 4

The truest, deepest prayer—that is,
spiritual communion with God—does not consist in
how much we know of doctrines or of spiritual truth.
True prayer consists in how much we are set free to love.

TERESA OF ÁVILA

20____ ....
....
....
....

20____ ....
....
....
....

20____ ....
....
....
....

20____ ....
....
....
....

20____ ....
....
....
....

July 5

I trust in you, LORD;
I say, "You are my God."
My times are in your hands.

PSALM 31:14–15 NIV

20___ ....
....
....
....

20___ ....
....
....
....

20___ ....
....
....
....

20___ ....
....
....
....

20___ ....
....
....
....

July 6

We reach for God in many ways. Through our pictures
and our prayers. Through our writing and our worship.
And through them He reaches us.

20___ ....
....
....
....

20___ ....
....
....
....

20___ ....
....
....
....

20___ ....
....
....
....

20___ ....
....
....
....

July 7

Children do not find it difficult or complicated
to talk to their parents, nor do they feel embarrassed to bring the
simplest need to their attention. Neither should we hesitate to
bring the simplest requests confidently to the Father.

RICHARD J. FOSTER

20___ ....
....
....
....

20___ ....
....
....
....

20___ ....
....
....
....

20___ ....
....
....
....

20___ ....
....
....
....

July 8

Look at the birds. They don't plant or harvest or
store food in barns, for your heavenly Father feeds them.
And aren't you far more valuable to him than they are?

MATTHEW 6:26 NLT

20____ ....
....
....
....

20____ ....
....
....
....

20____ ....
....
....
....

20____ ....
....
....
....

20____ ....
....
....
....

July 9

Open your hearts to the love God instills....
God loves you tenderly. What He gives you is not to be
kept under lock and key, but to be shared.

MOTHER TERESA

20____ ....
....
....
....

20____ ....
....
....
....

20____ ....
....
....
....

20____ ....
....
....
....

20____ ....
....
....
....

July 10

When I pray for another person, I am praying for God
to open my eyes so that I can see that person as God does,
and then enter into the stream of love that God
already directs toward that person.

PHILIP YANCEY

20___ ....
....
....
....

20___ ....
....
....
....

20___ ....
....
....
....

20___ ....
....
....
....

20___ ....
....
....
....

July 11

His burden is light, his yoke is easy. He carries
the heavy end of the load, always. I am just his "kid" carrying
what I can carry and he is a good Dad and never gives me a burden
that would discourage or harm me by its weight.

KATHERINE WALDEN

20___ ....
....
....
....

20___ ....
....
....
....

20___ ....
....
....
....

20___ ....
....
....
....

20___ ....
....
....
....

July 12

Come to me. Get away with me and you'll recover your life.
I'll show you how to take a real rest. Walk with me and work
with me—watch how I do it. Learn the unforced rhythms of grace.

MATTHEW 11:28–29 MSG

20____ ....
....
....
....

20____ ....
....
....
....

20____ ....
....
....
....

20____ ....
....
....
....

20____ ....
....
....
....

July 13

It takes some of us a lifetime to learn that Christ,
our Good Shepherd, knows exactly what He is doing with us.
He understands us perfectly.

PHILLIP KELLER

20___ ....
....
....
....

20___ ....
....
....
....
....

20___ ....
....
....
....

20___ ....
....
....
....

20___ ....
....
....
....

July 14

Nothing I do can make God love me more or less.
Nothing can separate me from His love!

20___ ....
....
....
....

20___ ....
....
....
....

20___ ....
....
....
....

20___ ....
....
....
....

20___ ....
....
....
....

July 15

To find God, you must look with all your heart.
To remain present to God, you must remain present to your heart.
To hear his voice, you must listen with all your heart.

JOHN ELDREDGE

20____ ....
....
....
....

20____ ....
....
....
....

20____ ....
....
....
....

20____ ....
....
....
....

20____ ....
....
....
....

July 16

If there is a God who speaks anywhere, surely He speaks here:
through waking up and working, through going away
and coming back again, through people you read
and books you meet, through falling asleep in the dark.

FREDERICK BUECHNER

20___ ....
....
....
....

20___ ....
....
....
....

20___ ....
....
....
....

20___ ....
....
....
....

20___ ....
....
....
....

July 17

—'Tis so sweet to trust in Jesus,
just to take Him at His Word;
just to rest upon His promise
and to know "Thus saith the Lord!"

Louisa M. R. Stead

20___ ....
....
....
....

20___ ....
....
....
....

20___ ....
....
....
....

20___ ....
....
....
....

20___ ....
....
....
....

July 18

Every word of God is flawless;
he is a shield to those who take refuge in him.

PROVERBS 30:5 NIV

20___ ....
....
....
....

20___ ....
....
....
....

20___ ....
....
....
....

20___ ....
....
....
....

20___ ....
....
....
....

July 19

You will reach your destination
if you walk with God.

20____ ....
....
....
....

20____ ....
....
....
....

20____ ....
....
....
....

20____ ....
....
....
....

20____ ....
....
....
....

July 20

Every evening I turn my worries over to God.
He's going to be up all night anyway.

MARY C. CROWLEY

20____ ....
....
....
....

20____ ....
....
....
....

20____ ....
....
....
....

20____ ....
....
....
....

20____ ....
....
....
....

July 21

The mystery of life is that the Lord of life cannot be known
except in and through the act of living. Without the concrete
and specific involvments of daily life we cannot come to know the
loving presence of Him who holds us in the palm of His hand.

HENRI J. M. NOUWEN

20___ ....
....
....
....

20___ ....
....
....
....

20___ ....
....
....
....

20___ ....
....
....
....

20___ ....
....
....
....

July 22

God loves each of us as
if there were only one of us.

AUGUSTINE

20___ ....
....
....
....

20___ ....
....
....
....

20___ ....
....
....
....

20___ ....
....
....
....

20___ ....
....
....
....

July 23

God understands our prayers even
when we can't find the words to say them.

20___ ....
....
....
....

20___ ....
....
....
....

20___ ....
....
....
....

20___ ....
....
....
....

20___ ....
....
....
....

July 24

Prayer is when you talk to God;
meditation is when you listen to God.

DIANA ROBINSON

20___ ....
....
....
....

20___ ....
....
....
....

20___ ....
....
....
....

20___ ....
....
....
....

20___ ....
....
....
....

July 25

God's promises are like the stars;
the darker the night the brighter they shine.

DAVID NICHOLAS

20____ ....
....
....
....

20____ ....
....
....
....

20____ ....
....
....
....

20____ ....
....
....
....

20____ ....
....
....
....

July 26

For all of God's promises have been fulfilled in Christ
with a resounding "Yes!" And through Christ, our "Amen"
(which means "Yes") ascends to God for his glory.

2 CORINTHIANS 1:20 NLT

20___ ....
....
....
....

20___ ....
....
....
....

20___ ....
....
....
....

20___ ....
....
....
....

20___ ....
....
....
....

July 27

Every morning I spend fifteen minutes
filling my mind full of God;
and so there's no room left for worry thoughts.

HOWARD CHANDLER CHRISTY

20___ ....
....
....
....

20___ ....
....
....
....

20___ ....
....
....
....

20___ ....
....
....
....

20___ ....
....
....
....

July 28

Because God is ever-present…He is always with me.
Because God knows everything…I will
go to Him with all my questions and concerns.

WILLIAM R. BRIGHT

20___

20___

20___

20___

20___

July 29

Faith comes from hearing the message,
and the message is heard through the word.

ROMANS 10:17 NIV

20___ ....
....
....
....

20___ ....
....
....
....

20___ ....
....
....
....

20___ ....
....
....
....

20___ ....
....
....
....

July 30

God writes with a pen that never blots, speaks with a tongue
that never slips, and acts with a hand that never fails.

HUBERT VAN ZELLER

20___ ....
....
....
....

20___ ....
....
....
....

20___ ....
....
....
....

20___ ....
....
....
....

20___ ....
....
....
....

July 31

Life from the Center is a life of unhurried peace and power.
It is simple. It is serene.... We need not get frantic.
He is at the helm. And when our little day is done,
we lie down quietly in peace, for all is well.

THOMAS R. KELLY

20___ ....
....
....
....

20___ ....
....
....
....

20___ ....
....
....
....

20___ ....
....
....
....

20___ ....
....
....
....

August 1

Jesus wants to live His life in you, to look through your eyes,
walk with your feet, love with your heart.

MOTHER TERESA

20___ ....
....
....
....

20___ ....
....
....
....

20___ ....
....
....
....

20___ ....
....
....
....

20___ ....
....
....
....

August 2

You will keep in perfect peace
all who trust in you,
all whose thoughts are fixed on you!

ISAIAH 26:3 NLT

20___ ....
....
....
....
....

20___ ....
....
....
....
....

20___ ....
....
....
....
....

20___ ....
....
....
....
....

20___ ....
....
....
....
....

August 3

He whose heart is kind beyond all measure,
Gives unto each day what He deems best,
Lovingly its part of pain and pleasure,
Mingling toil with peace and rest.

LINA SANDELL-BERG

20___ ....
....
....
....

20___ ....
....
....
....

20___ ....
....
....
....

20___ ....
....
....
....

20___ ....
....
....
....

August 4

God...will never speak to us through our circumstances in a way that contradicts His written Word. The Bible should be our first source of information when trying to discern the voice of God.

RON EDMONDSON

20___ ....
....
....
....

20___ ....
....
....
....

20___ ....
....
....
....

20___ ....
....
....
....

20___ ....
....
....
....

August 5

The word of God is living and powerful, and sharper
than any two-edged sword, piercing even to the division of soul
and spirit, and of joints and marrow, and is a discerner of
the thoughts and intents of the heart.

HEBREWS 4:12 NKJV

20____ ....
....
....
....

20____ ....
....
....
....

20____ ....
....
....
....

20____ ....
....
....
....

20____ ....
....
....
....

August 6

Through spending time in My presence,
you gain glimpses of My overflowing vastness.

SARAH YOUNG

20___ ....
....
....
....

20___ ....
....
....
....

20___ ....
....
....
....

20___ ....
....
....
....

20___ ....
....
....
....

August 7

Face the work of every day with the influence of a few thoughtful
quiet moments with your heart and God.

L. B. COWMAN

20___ ....
....
....
....

20___ ....
....
....
....

20___ ....
....
....
....

20___ ....
....
....
....

20___ ....
....
....
....

August 8

have your concert first, and then
r instrument afterwards. Begin the day
with the Word of God and prayer,
and get first of all into harmony with Him.

J. HUDSON TAYLOR

20____ ....
....
....
....

20____ ....
....
....
....

20____ ....
....
....
....

20____ ....
....
....
....

20____ ....
....
....
....

August 9

It is my belief that when you go ahead with your projects without praying and listening, it implies that you know better than God what needs to be done.

ANDREW RUDY

20___ ....
....
....
....

20___ ....
....
....
....

20___ ....
....
....
....

20___ ....
....
....
....

20___ ....
....
....
....

August 10

If we will commit our ways unto the Lord and trust Him,
He has promised that He would direct our paths.

DEBRA AIKEN

20___ ....
....
....
....

20___ ....
....
....
....

20___ ....
....
....
....

20___ ....
....
....
....

20___ ....
....
....
....

August 11

I will praise the LORD, who counsels me;
even at night my heart instructs me.

PSALM 16:7 NIV

20___ ....
....
....
....
....

20___ ....
....
....
....

20___ ....
....
....
....

20___ ....
....
....
....

20___ ....
....
....
....

August 12

Listening…means taking a vigorous, human interest in what is being told us. You can listen like a blank wall or like a splendid auditorium where every sound comes back fuller and richer.

ALICE DUER MILLER

20____ ....
....
....
....

20____ ....
....
....
....

20____ ....
....
....
....

20____ ....
....
....
....

20____ ....
....
....
....

August 13

If you know that God loves you, you should never
question a directive from Him.
It will always be right and best.

HENRY T. BLACKABY

20___ ....
....
....
....

20___ ....
....
....
....

20___ ....
....
....
....

20___ ....
....
....
....

20___ ....
....
....
....

August 14

This is my Father's world;
He shines in all that's fair.
In the rustling grass I hear Him pass;
He speaks to me everywhere.

MALTBIE D. BABCOCK

20____ ....
....
....
....

20____ ....
....
....
....

20____ ....
....
....
....

20____ ....
....
....
....

20____ ....
....
....
....

August 15

Let your faith…be in the quiet confidence that He will every day
and every moment keep you as the apple of His eye,
keep you in perfect peace and in the sure experience of
all the light and the strength you need.

ANDREW MURRAY

20___ ....
....
....
....

20___ ....
....
....
....

20___ ....
....
....
....

20___ ....
....
....
....

20___ ....
....
....
....

August 16

Keep me as the apple of Your eye;
hide me under the shadow of Your wings.

PSALM 17:8 NKJV

20___ ....
....
....
....

20___ ....
....
....
....

20___ ....
....
....
....

20___ ....
....
....
....

20___ ....
....
....
....

August 17

All happenings, great and small, are parables whereby God speaks.
The art of life is to get the message.

MALCOLM MUGGERIDGE

20___ ....
....
....
....

20___ ....
....
....
....

20___ ....
....
....
....

20___ ....
....
....
....

20___ ....
....
....
....

August 18

I believe the Bible is the best gift God has ever given to men.
All the good from the Savior of the world
is communicated to us through this book.

ABRAHAM LINCOLN

20____ ....
....
....
....

20____ ....
....
....
....

20____ ....
....
....
....

20____ ....
....
....
....

20____ ....
....
....
....

August 19

All Scripture is inspired by God and is useful to teach us what is
true and to make us realize what is wrong in our lives. It corrects
us when we are wrong and teaches us to do what is right.

2 TIMOTHY 3:16 NLT

20___ ....
....
....
....

20___ ....
....
....
....

20___ ....
....
....
....

20___ ....
....
....
....

20___ ....
....
....
....

August 20

If we knew how to listen, we would hear Him speaking to us.
For God does speak.... If we knew how to listen to God,
if we knew how to look around us,
our whole life would become prayer.

MICHAEL QUOIST

20___ ....
....
....
....

20___ ....
....
....
....

20___ ....
....
....
....

20___ ....
....
....
....

20___ ....
....
....
....

August 21

Rest is not idleness, and to lie sometimes on the grass
under the trees on a summer's day, listening to the murmur
of water, or watching the clouds float across the sky,
is by no means a waste of time.

SIR JOHN LUBBOCK

20___ ....
....
....
....

20___ ....
....
....
....

20___ ....
....
....
....

20___ ....
....
....
....

20___ ....
....
....
....

August 22

God walks with us.... He scoops us up in His arms or simply
sits with us in silent strength until we cannot avoid the awesome
recognition that yes, even now, He is here.

GLORIA GAITHER

20____ ....
....
....
....

20____ ....
....
....
....

20____ ....
....
....
....

20____ ....
....
....
....

20____ ....
....
....
....

August 23

Prayer is not overcoming God's reluctance,
but laying hold of His willingness.

MARTIN LUTHER

20___ ....
....
....
....

20___ ....
....
....
....

20___ ....
....
....
....

20___ ....
....
....
....

20___ ....
....
....
....

August 24

When I feel like I can't take another step or handle
one more problem, God says, "My grace is sufficient for you.
Lean on Me. Let Me be your strength."

20___ ....
....
....
....

20___ ....
....
....
....

20___ ....
....
....
....

20___ ....
....
....
....

20___ ....
....
....
....

August 25

I keep my eyes always on the LORD.
With him at my right hand, I will not be shaken.
Therefore my heart is glad and my tongue rejoices;
my body also will rest secure.

PSALM 16:8–9 NIV

20___ ....
....
....
....

20___ ....
....
....
....

20___ ....
....
....
....

20___ ....
....
....
....

20___ ....
....
....
....

August 26

You may pray for an hour and still not pray. You may meet God
for a moment and then be in touch with Him all day.

CARL FREDRIK WISLOFF

20___ ....
....
....
....

20___ ....
....
....
....

20___ ....
....
....
....

20___ ....
....
....
....

20___ ....
....
....
....

August 27

In prayer it is better to have a heart without words
than words without a heart.

JOHN BUNYAN

20___ ....
....
....
....

20___ ....
....
....
....

20___ ....
....
....
....

20___ ....
....
....
....

20___ ....
....
....
....

August 28

Only God can fully satisfy the hungry heart of man.

HUGH BLACK

20___ ....
....
....
....

20___ ....
....
....
....

20___ ....
....
....
....

20___ ....
....
....
....

20___ ....
....
....
....

August 29

God takes care of His own. He is moved by our weaknesses.
He stands ready to come to our rescue.
And at just the right moment He steps in
and proves Himself as our faithful heavenly Father.

CHARLES SWINDOLL

20___ ....
....
....
....

20___ ....
....
....
....

20___ ....
....
....
....

20___ ....
....
....
....

20___ ....
....
....
....

August 30

The LORD is close to the brokenhearted
and saves those who are crushed in spirit.

PSALM 34:18 NIV

20___ ....
....
....
....

20___ ....
....
....
....

20___ ....
....
....
....

20___ ....
....
....
....

20___ ....
....
....
....

August 31

Our God is at home with the rolling spheres,
and at home with broken hearts.

MANIE P. FERGUSON

20___ ....
....
....
....

20___ ....
....
....
....

20___ ....
....
....
....

20___ ....
....
....
....

20___ ....
....
....
....

September 1

Steep yourself in God-reality, God-initiative, God-provisions.
You'll find all your everyday human concerns will be met....
The Father wants to give you the very kingdom itself.

LUKE 12:31-32 MSG

20___ ....
....
....
....
....

20___ ....
....
....
....
....

20___ ....
....
....
....
....

20___ ....
....
....
....
....

20___ ....
....
....
....

September 2

Lord, hear my prayer. When I stumble over my words...listen
to my heart. I want to talk with You. I want to walk with You....
Take my hand and my heart and lead me in prayer..

MARILYN JANSEN

20___ ....
....
....
....

20___ ....
....
....
....

20___ ....
....
....
....

20___ ....
....
....
....

20___ ....
....
....
....

September 3

We encounter God in the ordinariness of life,
not in the search for spiritual highs and extraordinary,
mystical experiences, but in our simple presence in life.

BRENNAN MANNING

20___ ....

....

....

....

20___ ....

....

....

....

20___ ....

....

....

....

20___ ....

....

....

....

20___ ....

....

....

....

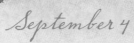

September 4

We do not understand the intricate pattern of the stars on their courses, but we know that He who created them does, and that just as surely as He guides them, He is charting a safe course for us.

BILLY GRAHAM

20___ ....
....
....
....

20___ ....
....
....
....

20___ ....
....
....
....

20___ ....
....
....
....

20___ ....
....
....
....

September 5

Get into the habit of saying, "Speak, Lord," and life will become a romance. Every time circumstances press in on you say, "Speak, Lord," and make time to listen.

OSWALD CHAMBERS

20___ ....
....
....
....

20___ ....
....
....
....

20___ ....
....
....
....

20___ ....
....
....
....

20___ ....
....
....
....

September 6

Serve only the LORD your God and fear him alone.
Obey his commands, listen to his voice, and cling to him.

DEUTERONOMY 13:4 NLT

20___ ....
....
....
....

20___ ....
....
....
....

20___ ....
....
....
....

20___ ....
....
....
....

20___ ....
....
....
....

September 7

A quiet morning with a loving God puts the events
of the upcoming day into proper perspective.

JANETTE OKE

20____ ....
....
....
....

20____ ....
....
....
....

20____ ....
....
....
....

20____ ....
....
....
....

20____ ....
....
....
....

September 8

Look up at all the stars in the night sky and hear your Father saying,
"I carefully set each one in its place.
Know that I love you more than these."

WENDY MOORE

20___ ....
....
....
....

20___ ....
....
....
....

20___ ....
....
....
....

20___ ....
....
....
....

20___ ....
....
....
....

September 9

Prayer becomes real when we grasp the reality and goodness of
God's constant presence with "the real me."

JOHN ORTBERG

20___

20___

20___

20___

20___

September 10

God speaks to us through His Spirit: God is not only
the Creator of all things and limitless in His abilities,
he is also intimate with his children,
speaking to us as we seek him for direction.

RON CHANNELL

20____ ....
....
....
....

20____ ....
....
....
....

20____ ....
....
....
....

20____ ....
....
....
....

20____ ....
....
....
....

September 11

We know that God causes everything to work together for the
good of those who love God and are called
according to his purpose for them.

ROMANS 8:28 NLT

20____ ....
....
....
....

20____ ....
....
....
....

20____ ....
....
....
....

20____ ....
....
....
....

20____ ....
....
....
....

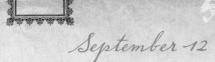

September 12

Walk and talk and work and laugh with your friends. But behind
the scenes, keep up the life of simple prayer and inward worship.

THOMAS R. KELLY

20___ ....
....
....
....

20___ ....
....
....
....

20___ ....
....
....
....

20___ ....
....
....
....

20___ ....
....
....
....

September 13

Beauty is God's handwriting.

CHARLES KINGSLEY

20____ ....
....
....
....

20____ ....
....
....
....

20____ ....
....
....
....

20____ ....
....
....
....

20____ ....
....
....
....

September 14

I believe in the sun even if it isn't shining.
I believe in love even when I am alone.
I believe in God even when He is silent.

20___ ....
....
....
....

20___ ....
....
....
....

20___ ....
....
....
....

20___ ....
....
....
....

20___ ....
....
....
....

September 15

Before me, even as behind, God is, and all is well.

JOHN GREENLEAF WHITTIER

20___ ....
....
....
....

20___ ....
....
....
....

20___ ....
....
....
....

20___ ....
....
....
....

20___ ....
....
....
....

September 16

The LORD confides in those who fear him;
he makes his covenant known to them.

PSALM 25:14 NIV

20___ ....
....
....
....

20___ ....
....
....
....

20___ ....
....
....
....

20___ ....
....
....
....

20___ ....
....
....
....

September 17

God is whispering, and sometimes shouting,
all through His Word, giving us instructions and principles for life.

REBECCA BARLOW JORDAN

20___ ....

....

....

....

20___ ....

....

....

....

20___ ....

....

....

....

20___ ....

....

....

....

20___ ....

....

....

....

September 18

Be assured, if you walk with Him and look to Him,
and expect help from Him, He will never fail you.

GEORGE MUELLER

20___ ....
....
....
....
....

20___ ....
....
....
....

20___ ....
....
....
....

20___ ....
....
....
....

20___ ....
....
....
....

September 19

God is not really "out there" at all. That restless heart, questioning
who you are and why you were created, that quiet voice that keeps
calling your name is not just out there, but dwells in you.

DAVID AND BARBARA SORENSEN

20___ ....
....
....
....

20___ ....
....
....
....

20___ ....
....
....
....

20___ ....
....
....
....

20___ ....
....
....
....

September 20

Heaven knows no difference between Sunday morning and Wednesday afternoon. God longs to speak as clearly in the workplace as He does in the sanctuary.

MAX LUCADO

20___ ....
....
....
....

20___ ....
....
....
....

20___ ....
....
....
....

20___ ....
....
....
....

20___ ....
....
....
....

September 21

The LORD's unfailing love surrounds the one who trusts in him.

PSALM 32:10 NIV

20___ ....
....
....
....

20___ ....
....
....
....

20___ ....
....
....
....

20___ ....
....
....

20___ ....
....
....

September 22

Lord, grant me a quiet mind,
That trusting Thee, for Thou art kind,
I may go on without a fear,
For Thou, my Lord, art always near.

AMY CARMICHAEL

20___ ....
....
....
....

20___ ....
....
....
....

20___ ....
....
....
....

20___ ....
....
....
....

20___ ....
....
....
....

September 23

God speaks to the crowd, but His call comes to individuals, and
through their personal obedience He acts.

PAUL TOURNIER

20____ ....

....

....

....

20____ ....

....

....

....

20____ ....

....

....

....

20____ ....

....

....

....

20____ ....

....

....

....

September 24

The voice of truth says, "Do not be afraid!"
And the voice of truth says, "This is for My glory."
Out of all the voices calling out to me,
I will choose to listen and believe the voice of truth.

MARK HALL AND STEVEN CURTIS CHAPMAN

20___ ....
....
....
....

20___ ....
....
....
....

20___ ....
....
....
....

20___ ....
....
....
....

20___ ....
....
....
....

September 25

To have God speak to the heart is a majestic experience,
an experience that people may miss if they monopolize
the conversation and never pause to hear God's responses.

CHARLES STANLEY

20___ ....
....
....
....

20___ ....
....
....
....

20___ ....
....
....
....

20___ ....
....
....
....

20___ ....
....
....
....

September 26

I will instruct you and teach you in the way you should go;
I will counsel you with my loving eye on you.

PSALM 32:8 NIV

20___ ....
....
....
....

20___ ....
....
....
....

20___ ....
....
....
....

20___ ....
....
....
....

20___ ....
....
....
....

September 27

You need not cry very loud;
he is nearer to us than we think.

BROTHER LAWRENCE

20___ ....
....
....
....

20___ ....
....
....
....

20___ ....
....
....
....

20___ ....
....
....
....

20___ ....
....
....
....

September 28

Some stand on tiptoe trying to reach God to talk to Him—
you try too hard, friend—drop to your knees and listen.
He'll hear you better that way.

TERRI GUILLEMETS

20___ ....
....
....
....

20___ ....
....
....
....

20___ ....
....
....
....

20___ ....
....
....
....

20___ ....
....
....
....

September 29

God speaks to us when we admit
we have absolutely nothing to say.

20___ ....
....
....
....

20___ ....
....
....
....

20___ ....
....
....
....

20___ ....
....
....
....

20___ ....
....
....
....

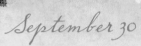

September 30

Whether you turn to the right or to the left, your ears will hear a
voice behind you, saying, "This is the way; walk in it."

ISAIAH 30:21 NIV

20___ ....
....
....
....

20___ ....
....
....
....

20___ ....
....
....
....

20___ ....
....
....
....

20___ ....
....
....
....

October 1

The lover of silence draws close to God.
He talks to Him in secret and God enlightens him.

JOHN CLIMACUS

20___ ....
....
....
....

20___ ....
....
....
....

20___ ....
....
....
....

20___ ....
....
....
....

20___ ....
....
....
....

October 2

Think back over your day and consider when God spoke. How did you sense it, or why did you fail to sense it at the time? It is often between the lines and in the empty places where we hear God.

LONNI COLLINS PRATT

20____

20____

20____

20____

20____

October 3

In waiting we begin to get in touch with the rhythms of life—
stillness and action, listening and decision. They are the
rhythms of God. It is in the everyday and the commonplace
that we learn patience, acceptance, and contentment.

RICHARD J. FOSTER

20___ ....
....
....
....

20___ ....
....
....
....

20___ ....
....
....
....

20___ ....
....
....
....

20___ ....
....
....
....

October 4

Tuck [this] thought into your heart today. Treasure it. Your Father
God cares about your daily everythings that concern you.

KAY ARTHUR

20___ ....
....
....
....

20___ ....
....
....
....

20___ ....
....
....
....

20___ ....
....
....
....

20___ ....
....
....
....

October 5

The eyes of the LORD are on those who fear him,
on those whose hope is in his unfailing love.

PSALM 33:18 NIV

20___

20___

20___

20___

20___

October 6

Be still in my presence, even though countless tasks clamor for your attention. Nothing is as important as spending time with Me.

SARAH YOUNG

20___ ....
....
....
....

20___ ....
....
....
....

20___ ....
....
....
....

20___ ....
....
....
....

20___ ....
....
....
....

October 7

Reading about nature is fine, but if a person walks in the woods
and listens carefully, he can learn more than what is in books,
for they speak with the voice of God.

GEORGE WASHINGTON CARVER

20___ ....
....
....
....

20___ ....
....
....
....

20___ ....
....
....
....

20___ ....
....
....
....

20___ ....
....
....
....

October 8

We need to find God, and He cannot be found in noise
and restlessness. God is the friend of silence. See how nature…
grows in silence…. We need silence to be able to touch souls.

MOTHER TERESA

20___ ....
....
....
....

20___ ....
....
....
....

20___ ....
....
....
....

20___ ....
....
....
....

20___ ....
....
....
....

October 9

Teach me to do Your will,
For You are my God;
Let Your good Spirit lead me on level ground.

Psalm 143:10 NASB

20____

20____

20____

20____

20____

October 10

Lord God, I long to hear Your voice but not just secondhand
through teachers, as wonderful and godly as they can be.
I long to hear Your voice firsthand.

SHEILA WALSH

20___ ....
....
....
....

20___ ....
....
....
....

20___ ....
....
....
....

20___ ....
....
....
....

20___ ....
....
....
....

October 11

Sometimes it is necessary for us to speak.
At other times it is important that we be quiet.
Wisdom comes with knowing the difference.

Mrs. D. E. Clay

20___ ....
....
....
....

20___ ....
....
....
....

20___ ....
....
....
....

20___ ....
....
....
....

20___ ....
....
....
....

October 12

To pray is to listen to the One who calls you
"my beloved daughter," "my beloved son," "my beloved child."
To pray is to let that voice speak to the center of your being,
to your guts, and let that voice resound in your whole being.

HENRI J. M. NOUWEN

20___ ....
....
....
....

20___ ....
....
....
....

20___ ....
....
....
....

20___ ....
....
....
....

20___ ....
....
....
....

October 13

When I can't figure something out,
God says, "Trust me to guide you and direct your steps."

20___ ....
....
....
....

20___ ....
....
....
....

20___ ....
....
....
....

20___ ....
....
....
....

20___ ....
....
....
....

October 14

Your word is a lamp for my feet,
a light on my path.

PSALM 119:105 NIV

20___ ....
....
....
....

20___ ....
....
....
....

20___ ....
....
....
....

20___ ....
....
....
....

20___ ....
....
....
....

October 15

If we do not listen we do not come to the truth. If we do not pray
we do not even get as far as listening.... Four things go together:
silence, listening, prayer, truth.

HUBERT VAN ZELLER

20___ ....
....
....
....

20___ ....
....
....
....

20___ ....
....
....
....

20___ ....
....
....
....

20___ ....
....
....
....

October 16

When I find myself racing around, trying to fill a day with mindless tasks or petty entertainment, this is usually the time that God whispers to my heart to draw away with Him and to silence my heart as He wishes to speak.

KATHERINE WALDEN

20___ ....
....
....
....

20___ ....
....
....
....

20___ ....
....
....
....

20___ ....
....
....
....

20___ ....
....
....
....

October 17

When I'm feeling unlovable and unlovely, the Lord reminds me,
"I have loved you with an everlasting love."

20___ ....
....
....
....

20___ ....
....
....
....

20___ ....
....
....
....

20___ ....
....
....
....

20___ ....
....
....
....

October 18

Is there a random act of kindness you feel
the Lord might be leading you to do today?

20___ ....
....
....
....

20___ ....
....
....
....

20___ ....
....
....
....

20___ ....
....
....
....

20___ ....
....
....
....

October 19

The grass withers and the flowers fade,
but the word of our God stands forever.

ISAIAH 40:8 NLT

20___ ....
....
....
....

20___ ....
....
....
....

20___ ....
....
....
....

20___ ....
....
....
....

20___ ....
....
....
....

October 20

We would be better Christians if we were…
waiting upon God and gathering through meditation on His Word
spiritual strength for labor in His service.

CHARLES SPURGEON

20____

20____

20____

20____

20____

October 21

When my legs get restless and I grow impatient,
God whispers to me, "Just wait and see what I have planned."

20____ ....
....
....
....

20____ ....
....
....
....

20____ ....
....
....
....

20____ ....
....
....
....

20____ ....
....
....
....

October 22

What God says is best, is best,
though all the men in the world are against it.

JOHN BUNYAN

20____ ....
....
....
....

20____ ....
....
....

20____ ....
....
....
....

20____ ....
....
....

20____ ....
....
....
....

October 23

Our days are full of nonsense, and yet not,
because it is precisely into the nonsense of our days that God
speaks to us words of great significance.

FREDERICK BUECHNER

20___ ....
....
....
....

20___ ....
....
....
....

20___ ....
....
....
....

20___ ....
....
....
....

20___ ....
....
....
....

October 24

If you make yourselves at home with me and my words
are at home in you, you can be sure that whatever you ask
will be listened to and acted upon.

JOHN 15:7 MSG

20___ ....
....
....
....

20___ ....
....
....
....

20___ ....
....
....
....

20___ ....
....
....
....

20___ ....
....
....
....

October 25

When a problem looks insurmountable, God whispers,
"Nothing is impossible for Me."

20___ ....
....
....
....

20___ ....
....
....
....

20___ ....
....
....
....

20___ ....
....
....

20___ ....
....
....
....

October 26

All this beauty exists so you and I can see His glory, His artwork.
It's like an invitation to worship Him, to know Him.

DONALD MILLER

20_____ ....
....
....
....

20_____ ....
....
....
....

20_____ ....
....
....
....

20_____ ....
....
....
....

20_____ ....
....
....
....

October 27

While we have been pursuing God He has been rushing toward us
with reckless love, arms flung wide to hug us home.

KEN GIRE

20____

....

....

....

20____

....

....

....

20____

....

....

....

20____

....

....

....

20____

....

....

....

October 28

God's friendship is the unexpected joy we find
when we reach for His outstretched hand.

JANET L. SMITH

20___ ....

....

....

....

20___ ....

....

....

....

20___ ....

....

....

20___ ....

....

....

....

20___ ....

....

....

....

October 29

You alone are the LORD. You made the heavens,
even the highest heavens, and all their starry host,
the earth and all that is on it, the seas and all that is in them.
You give life to everything.

NEHEMIAH 9:6 NIV

20____ ....
....
....
....

20____ ....
....
....
....

20____ ....
....
....
....

20____ ....
....
....
....

20____ ....
....
....
....

October 30

Whenever I see sunbeams coming through clouds, it always
looks to me like God shining Himself down onto us.
The thing about sunbeams is they're always there
even though you can't see them. Same with God.

TERRI GUILLEMETS

20____ ....
....
....
....

20____ ....
....
....
....

20____ ....
....
....
....

20____ ....
....
....
....

20____ ....
....
....
....

October 31

We don't earn God's love; we receive it.
We don't work for His approval; He approves us.

DILLON BURROUGHS

20___

20___

20___

20___

20___

November 1

When I feel alone, the Lord tells me,
"I will never leave you or forsake you."

20____ ....
....
....
....

20____ ....
....
....
....

20____ ....
....
....
....

20____ ....
....
....
....

20____ ....
....
....
....

November 2

Sometimes our circumstances may look gloomy,
but we haven't heard the truth of our circumstances
until we have heard from God.

20____ ....
....
....
....

20____ ....
....
....
....

20____ ....
....
....
....

20____ ....
....
....
....

20____ ....
....
....
....

November 3

The words I have spoken to you—
they are full of the Spirit and life.

JOHN 6:63 NIV

20____ ....
....
....
....

20____ ....
....
....
....

20____ ....
....
....
....

20____ ....
....
....
....

20____ ....
....
....
....

November 4

God does not waste our time…. Every experience
and person can lead us to God, and God is waiting to be found in
each moment of our day, waiting for us to allow the things and
people around us to cause us to remember him.

MIA POHLMAN

20___ ....

....

....

....

20___ ....

....

....

....

20___ ....

....

....

....

20___ ....

....

....

....

20___ ....

....

....

....

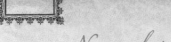

November 5

Are you dealing with a disappointment, something that didn't
work out the way you'd hoped? Take it to the Lord. Let Him speak
words of comfort, hope, and reassurance that He will work all
things for your good.

20____ ....
....
....
....
....

20____ ....
....
....
....
....

20____ ....
....
....
....
....

20____ ....
....
....
....
....

20____ ....
....
....
....

November 6

It is better to trust in the Lord than to put confidence in man
because God is all-powerful. The things which are
impossible with man are possible with God.

DEBRA AIKEN

20___ ....
....
....
....

20___ ....
....
....
....

20___ ....
....
....
....

20___ ....
....
....
....

20___ ....
....
....
....

November 7

When you're still in your soul you put yourself in a position
to connect with God and others. And to give and receive love is
what life is all about.

BILL GAULTIERE

20___ ....
....
....
....

20___ ....
....
....
....

20___ ....
....
....
....

20___ ....
....
....
....

20___ ....
....
....
....

November 8

Teach me to let go, dear God, and pray undisturbed until
My heart is filled with inner peace and I learn to know your will.

HELEN STEINER RICE

20___ ....
....
....
....

20___ ....
....
....
....

20___ ....
....
....
....

20___ ....
....
....
....

20___ ....
....
....
....

November 9

Let God's promises shine on your problems.

CORRIE TEN BOOM

20___ ....
....
....
....

20___ ....
....
....
....

20___ ....
....
....
....

20___ ....
....
....
....

20___ ....
....
....
....

November 10

Search me, God, and know my heart;
test me and know my anxious thoughts.

PSALM 139:23 NIV

20___ ....
....
....
....

20___ ....
....
....
....

20___ ....
....
....
....

20___ ....
....
....
....

20___ ....
....
....
....

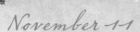

November 11

Almighty God, in whose hands lies the destiny of men and nations,
let not the hopes of men perish, nor the sacrifices of men
be in vain.... Draw us, O Lord, towards loving kindness
and guide us into the way of peace.

20___ ....
....
....
....

20___ ....
....
....
....

20___ ....
....
....
....

20___ ....
....
....
....

20___ ....
....
....
....

November 12

Answered prayer is the interchange of love
between the Father and His child.

ANDREW MURRAY

20___ ....
....
....
....

20___ ....
....
....
....

20___ ....
....
....
....

20___ ....
....
....
....

20___ ....
....
....
....

November 13

To place ourselves in range of God's choicest gifts, we have to
walk with God, work with God, lean on God, cling to God,
come to have the sense and feel of God, refer all things to God.

CORNELIUS PLANTINGA JR.

20___ ....
....
....
....

20___ ....
....
....
....

20___ ....
....
....
....

20___ ....
....
....
....

20___ ....
....
....
....

November 14

I know Him because He first knew me, and continues to know me.
He knows me as a friend, One who loves me;
and there is no moment when His eye is off me,
or His attention distracted from me.

J. I. PACKER

20___ ....
....
....
....

20___ ....
....
....
....

20___ ....
....
....
....

20___ ....
....
....
....

20___ ....
....
....
....

November 15

I sing because I'm happy,
I sing because I'm free,
For His eye is on the sparrow,
And I know He watches me.

CIVILLA MARTIN

20___ ....
....
....
....

20___ ....
....
....
....

20___ ....
....
....
....

20___ ....
....
....
....

20___ ....
....
....
....

November 16

The LORD is my shepherd, I lack nothing.
He makes me lie down in green pastures,
he leads me beside quiet waters.

PSALM 23:1–2 NIV

20___ ....
....
....
....

20___ ....
....
....
....

20___ ....
....
....
....

20___ ....
....
....
....

20___ ....
....
....
....

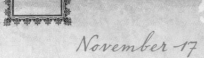

November 17

Trust the past to God's mercy,
the present to God's love,
and the future to God's providence.

AUGUSTINE

20___ ....
....
....
....

20___ ....
....
....
....

20___ ....
....
....
....

20___ ....
....
....
....

20___ ....
....
....
....

November 18

You can't analyze God. He is too awesome, too big,
too mysterious. I know now, Lord, why you utter no answer.
You Yourself are the answer.

C. S. Lewis

20___ ....
....
....
....

20___ ....
....
....
....

20___ ....
....
....
....

20___ ....
....
....
....

20___ ....
....
....
....

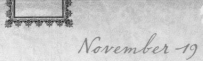

November 19

I know the Lord is always with me.
I will not be shaken, for he is right beside me.

Psalm 16:8 nlt

20___ ....
....
....
....

20___ ....
....
....
....

20___ ....
....
....
....

20___ ....
....
....
....

20___ ....
....
....
....

November 20

Stillness is a state of calm. Nothing brings calm like prayer,
nor will anything restore your peace
like the quietness of conversation with God.

20___ ....
....
....
....

20___ ....
....
....
....

20___ ....
....
....
....

20___ ....
....
....
....

20___ ....
....
....
....

November 21

I found the bread in my kitchen this morning, Lord. I thank You.
I found the fresh air as I stood outside the door. I praise You.
For all that I see that You do for me, I thank You. For all that
I do not see that You do for me, I praise You.

CHRISTOPHER DE VINCK

20___ ....

....

....

....

20___ ....

....

....

....

20___ ....

....

....

....

20___ ....

....

....

....

20___ ....

....

....

....

November 22

Almighty…God, thank You for paying attention to small things.
Thank You for valuing the insignificant. Thank You for
being interested in the lilies of the field and the birds of the air.
Thank You for caring about me. Amen.

RICHARD J. FOSTER

20___ ....
....
....
....

20___ ....
....
....
....

20___ ....
....
....
....

20___ ....
....
....
....

20___ ....
....
....
....

November 23

The wonder of our Lord is that He is so accessible to us
in the common things of our lives: the cup of water...welcoming
children into our arms...fellowship over a meal...giving thanks.

NANCIE CARMICHAEL

20___ ....
....
....
....

20___ ....
....
....
....

20___ ....
....
....
....

20___ ....
....
....
....

20___ ....
....
....
....

November 24

Always be joyful. Never stop praying.
Be thankful in all circumstances,
for this is God's will for you.

1 Thessalonians 5:16-18 nlt

20___ ....
....
....
....

20___ ....
....
....
....

20___ ....
....
....
....

20___ ....
....
....
....

20___ ....
....
....
....

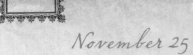

November 25

O Lord my God, thank You for bringing this day to a close;
Thank You for giving me rest in body and soul.

DIETRICH BONHOEFFER

20___ ....
....
....
....

20___ ....
....
....
....

20___ ....
....
....
....

20___ ....
....
....
....

20___ ....
....
....
....

November 26

A single grateful thought towards heaven
is the most perfect prayer.

G. E. LESSING

20____ ....
....
....
....

20____ ....
....
....
....

20____ ....
....
....
....

20____ ....
....
....
....

20____ ....
....
....
....

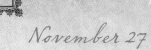

November 27

Those blessings are sweetest that are won
with prayer and worn with thanks.

THOMAS GOODWIN

20___ ....
....
....
....

20___ ....
....
....
....

20___ ....
....
....
....

20___ ....
....
....
....

20___ ....
....
....
....

November 28

We would worry less if we praised more.

HARRY IRONSIDE

20____ ....
....
....
....

20____ ....
....
....
....

20____ ....
....
....
....

20____ ....
....
....
....

20____ ....
....
....
....

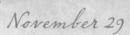

November 29

The LORD is my strength and shield.
I trust him with all my heart.
He helps me, and my heart is filled with joy.
I burst out in songs of thanksgiving.

PSALM 28:7 NLT

20___ ....

....

....

....

20___ ....

....

....

....

20___ ....

....

....

....

20___ ....

....

....

....

20___ ....

....

....

....

November 30

All God's glory and beauty come from within,
and there He delights to dwell. His visits there are frequent,
His conversation sweet, His comforts refreshing,
His peace passing all understanding.

THOMAS A KEMPIS

20___ ....
....
....
....

20___ ....
....
....
....

20___ ....
....
....
....

20___ ....
....
....
....

20___ ....
....
....
....

December 1

God is talking to you. His whispers are in advice from your family,
the actions of a friend, the lines of a poem. Just listen.

20____ ....
....
....
....

20____ ....
....
....
....

20____ ....
....
....
....

20____ ....
....
....
....

20____ ....
....
....
....

December 2

Biblically, waiting is not just something we
have to do until we get what we want. Waiting is part
of the process of becoming what God wants us to be.

JOHN ORTBERG

20___ ....
....
....
....

20___ ....
....
....
....

20___ ....
....
....
....

20___ ....
....
....
....

20___ ....
....
....
....

December 3

When my anxious thoughts multiply within me,
Your consolations delight my soul.

PSALM 94:19 NASB

20___ ....
....
....
....

20___ ....
....
....
....

20___ ....
....
....
....

20___ ....
....
....
....

20___ ....
....
....
....

December 4

Perhaps one of the ways I can sense
God's presence the most and "hear" His voice the best
is when I am praising Him through music.

REBECCA BARLOW JORDAN

20___ ....
....
....
....

20___ ....
....
....
....

20___ ....
....
....
....

20___ ....
....
....
....

20___ ....
....
....
....

December 5

Trusting God completely means having faith that
He knows what is best for your life. You expect Him
to keep His promises, help you with problems,
and do the impossible when necessary.

RICK WARREN

20___ ....
....
....
....

20___ ....
....
....
....

20___ ....
....
....
....

20___ ....
....
....
....

20___ ....
....
....
....

December 6

The LORD your God…will rejoice over you with gladness,
He will quiet you with His love,
He will rejoice over you with singing.

ZEPHANIAH 3:17 NKJV

20____ ....

20____ ....

20____ ....

20____ ....

20____ ....

December 7

Think back to a time when God spoke to you. Do you remember
what He said? As we listen, our ears become more sensitive, and
like Jesus, we will hear God all the time.

OSWALD CHAMBERS

20___ ....
....
....
....

20___ ....
....
....
....

20___ ....
....
....
....

20___ ....
....
....
....

20___ ....
....
....
....

December 8

What extraordinary delight we find in the presence of God.
He draws us in, His welcome so fresh and inviting
we cannot help but hear His heart.

20___ ....
....
....
....

20___ ....
....
....
....

20___ ....
....
....
....

20___ ....
....
....
....

20___ ....
....
....
....

December 9

Know that the LORD your God, He is God, the faithful God who
keeps covenant and mercy for a thousand generations with those
who love Him and keep His commandments.

DEUTERONOMY 7:9 NKJV

20___ ....
....
....
....

20___ ....
....
....
....

20___ ....
....
....
....

20___ ....
....
....
....

20___ ....
....
....
....

December 10

Approach Christmas with an expectant hush,
rather than a last-minute rush.

20___ ....
....
....
....

20___ ....
....
....
....

20___ ....
....
....
....

20___ ....
....
....
....

20___ ....
....
....
....

December 11

Trust God where you cannot trace Him. Do not try to penetrate the cloud He brings over you; rather look to the bow that is on it. The mystery is God's; the promise is yours.

JOHN MACDUFF

20___ ....
....
....
....

20___ ....
....
....
....

20___ ....
....
....
....

20___ ....
....
....
....

20___ ....
....
....
....

December 12

Prayer is not asking. Prayer is putting oneself
in the hands of God, at His disposition, and listening to His voice
in the depths of our hearts.

MOTHER TERESA

20____ ....
....
....
....

20____ ....
....
....
....

20____ ....
....
....
....

20____ ....
....
....
....

20____ ....
....
....
....

December 13

It is for our good, individually and collectively,
to live our lives in interactive dependence upon God.

BRENNAN MANNING

20___ ....
....
....
....

20___ ....
....
....
....

20___ ....
....
....
....

20___ ....
....
....
....

20___ ....
....
....
....

December 14

Behold, the virgin shall be with child, and bear a Son, and they
shall call His name Immanuel…God with us.

MATTHEW 1:23 NKJV

20___ ....

....

....

....

20___ ....

....

....

....

20___ ....

....

....

....

20___ ....

....

....

....

20___ ....

....

....

....

December 15

This is the great mystery of Christmas that continues to give us comfort and consolation: we are not alone on our journey.

HENRI J. M. NOUWEN

20___ ....
....
....
....

20___ ....
....
....
....

20___ ....
....
....
....

20___ ....
....
....
....

20___ ....
....
....
....

December 16

Begin to talk to the Lord Jesus today and get to know him.
He's the difference-maker. He will meet the needs
in your life in ways that will astound you.

RON CHANNELL

20____ ....
....
....
....

20____ ....
....
....
....

20____ ....
....
....
....

20____ ....
....
....
....

20____ ....
....
....
....

December 17

For a child will be born to us, a son will be given to us;
And the government will rest on His shoulders;
And His name will be called Wonderful Counselor,
Mighty God, Eternal Father, Prince of Peace.

ISAIAH 9:6 NASB

20___ ....
....
....
....

20___ ....
....
....
....

20___ ....
....
....
....

20___ ....
....
....
....

20___ ....
....
....
....

December 18

The Lord has promised to show us great and mighty things when
we call upon Him. He does great and unsearchable things and
marvelous things without number.

DEBRA AIKEN

20___ ....
....
....
....

20___ ....
....
....
....

20___ ....
....
....
....

20___ ....
....
....
....

20___ ....
....
....
....

December 19

God sent a star to light the night for The Way, The Truth,
The Life—His Son. He sent the Light of Life to prove His heart so
we would invite His Son into our own.

PAMELA DOWD

20___ ....
....
....
....

20___ ....
....
....
....

20___ ....
....
....
....

20___ ....
....
....
....

20___ ....
....
....

December 20

Love came down at Christmas,
Love all lovely, Love divine;
Love was born at Christmas;
Star and angels gave the sign.

CHRISTINA ROSSETTI

20_____ ....
....
....
....

20_____ ....
....
....
....

20_____ ....
....
....
....

20_____ ....
....
....
....

20_____ ....
....
....
....

December 21

God's gifts put man's best dreams to shame.

ELIZABETH BARRETT BROWNING

20___ ....
....
....
....

20___ ....
....
....
....

20___ ....
....
....
....

20___ ....
....
....
....

20___ ....
....
....
....

December 22

Love has a name. *Jesus.*
Love has a place. Our hearts.
Love has a story.
And it's not finished yet.

20____ ....
....
....
....

20____ ....
....
....
....

20____ ....
....
....
....

20____ ....
....
....
....

20____ ....
....
....
....

December 23

This is Christmas: not the tinsel, not the giving and receiving,
not even the carols, but the humble heart that receives anew
the wondrous gift, the Christ.

FRANK MCKIBBEN

20___ ....
....
....
....

20___ ....
....
....
....

20___ ....
....
....
....

20___ ....
....
....
....

20___ ....
....
....
....

December 24

If we could condense all the truths of Christmas
into only three words, these would be the words: "God with us."

JOHN MACARTHUR

20___ ....
....
....
....
....

20___ ....
....
....
....
....

20___ ....
....
....
....
....

20___ ....
....
....
....
....

20___ ....
....
....
....
....

December 25

Best of all, Christmas means a spirit of love,
a time when the love of God and love of our fellow man
should prevail...a time when our thoughts and deeds and the spirit
of our lives manifest the presence of God.

GEORGE F. McDOUGALL

20___ ....
....
....
....

20___ ....
....
....
....

20___ ....
....
....
....

20___ ....
....
....
....

20___ ....
....
....
....

December 26

Perhaps this moment is unclear.... Trust that God will
help you work it out, and that all the unclear moments
will bring you to that moment of clarity and action when you are
known by Him and know Him.

WENDY MOORE

20___ ....
....
....
....

20___ ....
....
....
....

20___ ....
....
....
....

20___ ....
....
....
....

20___ ....
....
....
....

December 27

God's silence is in no way indicative of His activity or involvement
in our lives. He may be silent but He is not still.

CHARLES STANLEY

20___ ....
....
....
....

20___ ....
....
....
....

20___ ....
....
....
....

20___ ....
....
....
....

20___ ....
....
....
....

December 28

I speak to you from the depths of your being. Hear Me saying soothing words of peace, assuring you of My love.

Sarah Young

20___ ....
....
....
....

20___ ....
....
....
....

20___ ....
....
....
....

20___ ....
....
....
....

20___ ....
....
....
....

December 29

God bless you and utterly satisfy your heart…with Himself.

AMY CARMICHAEL

20___ ....
....
....
....
....

20___ ....
....
....
....

20___ ....
....
....
....

20___ ....
....
....
....

20___ ....
....
....
....

December 30

Ask me and I will tell you remarkable secrets
you do not know about things to come.

JEREMIAH 33:3 NLT

20____ ....
....
....
....

20____ ....
....
....
....

20____ ....
....
....
....

20____ ....
....
....
....

20____ ....
....
....
....

December 31

Listen to your life. See it for the fathomless mystery that it is.
In the boredom and pain of it no less than in the
excitement and gladness...because in the last analysis
all moments are key moments and life itself is grace.

FREDERICK BUECHNER

20___

20___

20___

20___

20___

Ellie Claire® Gift & Paper Corp.
Brentwood, TN 37027
EllieClaire.com
A Worthy Publishing Company

When God Speaks, Take Good Notes
Five-Year Journal
© 2013 by Ellie Claire Gift & Paper Corp.

ISBN 978-1-60936-836-4

Excluding Scripture verses and deity pronouns, in some quotations references to
men and masculine pronouns have been replaced with gender-neutral or feminine
references. Additionally, in some quotations we have carefully updated verb forms
and wording that may distract modern readers.

Stock or custom editions of Ellie Claire titles may be purchased in bulk
for educational, business, ministry, fundraising, or sales promotional use.
For information, please e-mail info@EllieClaire.com

Compiled by Jill Jones.
Cover and interior design by Studio Gearbox | studiogearbox.com.
Typesetting by Jeff Jansen | aestheticsoup.net

Printed in China
1 2 3 4 5 6 7 8 9 – 18 17 16 15 14 13